How to use e

Issue 108

The 92 daily readings in this issue of *Explore* are designed to help you understand and apply the Bible as you read it each day.

It's serious!

We suggest that you allow 15 minutes each day to work through the Bible passage with the notes. It should be a meal, not a snack! Readings from other parts of the Bible can throw valuable light on the study passage. These cross-references can be skipped if you are already feeling full up, but will expand your grasp of the Bible. *Explore* uses the NIV2011 Bible translation, but you can also use it with the NIV1984 or ESV translations.

Sometimes a prayer box will encourage you to stop and pray through the lessons—but it is always important to allow time to pray for God's Spirit to bring his word to life, and to shape the way we think and live through it.

We're serious!

All of us who work on *Explore* share a passion for getting the Bible into people's lives. We fiercely hold to the Bible as God's word—to honour and follow, not to explain away.

1 Find a time you can read the Bible each day

2 Find a place where you can be quiet and think

3 Ask God to help you understand

4 Carefully read through the Bible passage for today

5 Study the verses with *Explore*, taking time to think

6 Pray about what you have read

thegoodbook
COMPANY

BIBLICAL | RELEVANT | ACCESSIBLE

Welcome to **explore**

Being a Christian isn't a skill you learn, nor is it a lifestyle choice. It's about having a real relationship with the living God through his Son, Jesus Christ. The Bible tells us that this relationship is like a marriage.

It's important to start with this, because it is easy to view the practice of daily Bible reading as a Christian duty, or a hard discipline that is just one more thing to get done in our busy lives.

But the Bible is God speaking to us: opening his mind to us on how he thinks, what he wants for us and what his plans are for the world. And most importantly, it tells us what he has done for us in sending his Son, Jesus Christ, into the world. It's the way that the Spirit shows Jesus to us, and changes us as we behold his glory.

Here are a few suggestions for making your time with God more of a joy than a burden:

- *Time:* Find a time when you will not be disturbed. Many people have found that the morning is the best time as it sets you up for the day. But whatever works for you is right for you.

- *Place:* Jesus says that we are not to make a great show of our religion *(see Matthew 6:5-6)*, but rather, to pray with the door to our room shut. Some people plan to get to work a few minutes earlier and get their Bible out in an office or some other quiet corner.

- *Prayer:* Although *Explore* helps with specific prayer ideas from the passage, do try to develop your own lists to pray through. Use the flap inside the back cover to help with this. And allow what you read in the Scriptures to shape what you pray for yourself, the world and others.

- *Feast:* You can use the "Bible in a year" line at the bottom of each page to help guide you through the entire Scriptures throughout 2024. This year, the passages each day are linked, showing how God makes and keeps his promises. We're grateful to Katherine Fedor of treasureinthebible.com for her permission to use this Bible-reading plan. You'll find passages to read six days a week—Sunday is a "day off", or a day to catch up!

- *Share:* As the saying goes, *expression deepens impression.* So try to cultivate the habit of sharing with others what you have learned. Why not join our Facebook group to share your encouragements, questions and prayer requests? Search for *Explore: For your daily walk with God.*

And enjoy it! As you read God's word and God's Spirit works in your mind and your heart, you are going to see Jesus, and appreciate more of his love for you and his promises to you. That's amazing!

Carl Laferton is the Editorial Director of The Good Book Company

ROMANS: Free

We return to the book of Romans, and to one of the best-loved chapters in the whole of Scripture…

Through Christ Jesus

Read Romans 7:25b – 8:2

> ❷ *What does 8:1 tell us about being "in Christ"? Why is this wonderful news?*
>
> ❷ *What else has happened to Christians (v 2)?*

···· **TIME OUT** ···································

The phrase Paul uses in verse 1 is much stronger than simply saying we are not condemned; it is that there is no condemnation at all—no possibility of it. Not only are we not condemned, we can never and will never be condemned.

> ❷ *How does this affect our response to sin?*
>
> ❷ *How does this affect our view of our future?*

···

In chapter 7, Paul showed us that Christians still wrestle with remaining, indwelling sin—"what I hate I *do*" (7:15). Yet at the same time, Christians now experience a real disgust over sin—"what I *hate* I do".

Although they sin, for those who are "in Christ Jesus" there "is now no condemnation"—first, not because of their own obedience (chapter 7 has shown that no Christian obeys as they should), but because of the work of God's Son and God's Spirit (8:2). And second, because the Spirit now works to do what we cannot—overcome sin. The work of the Spirit is what chapter 8 is about.

His own Son

Read Romans 8:3-4

> ❷ *Why couldn't the law free us from death (v 3)?*
>
> ❷ *How did God achieve it (v 3)?*
>
> ❷ *He did this in order to achieve what?*

In his Son, God has defeated the legal penalty of sin—death. But this is not all: through his Son's work, God now sends the Spirit to his people, to wipe out sin in our lives. "The righteous requirement of the law" can now "be fully met in us" (v 4). How can this be? Because we "do not live according to the flesh but according to the Spirit".

Verse 4 is telling us that everything Christ did for us—his incarnation, life, death and resurrection—was "in order that" we would live a holy life. Jesus' whole purpose was to make us holy, and able to live holy lives. This is the greatest possible motive for living a holy life. Whenever we sin, we are endeavouring to frustrate the aim and purpose of the entire ministry of Christ Jesus. If this doesn't work as an incentive for living a holy life, nothing will.

❤ Apply

> ❷ *In what part of your life do you need to let this truth change you today?*

Minding the mind

What we dwell on in our minds will shape the way we live our lives. What you set your mind on shapes your character and behaviour.

Setting our minds

Read Romans 8:5-8

> ❷ *What are the two things people can "set" their minds on (v 5)?*

To set your mind is more than simply thinking about something. It means to focus intently on something, to be preoccupied with it, to let your attention and imagination be totally captured by something. Wherever your mind goes most naturally and freely when there is nothing else to distract it— that is what you really live for.

···· **TIME OUT** ···

> ❷ *What do you do with your solitude?*
>
> ❷ *What does this suggest your mind is set on?*

The realm of the Spirit

Read Romans 8:9-14

> ❷ *Who is controlled by the Spirit (v 9, first sentence)?*
>
> ❷ *Who has the Spirit (v 9, 2nd sentence)?*
>
> ❷ *What is true of the Christian...*
> • *now (v 10)?*
> • *in the future (v 11)?*
>
> ❷ *What do Christians therefore have an obligation to do (v 12)?*

Christians are not those who live by the sinful nature (or "flesh") and therefore die (v 13); we will, and must be, those who "put to death the misdeeds of the body". Paul is saying that we have been made alive (v 10), and we will one day have renewed bodies (v 11); and for now, we put to death the sinful nature, in the power of the Spirit.

This means a ruthless, full-hearted resistance to sinful practice. "Put to death" is a violent, sweeping phrase—it means to declare war on attitudes and behaviours that are wrong. A Christian doesn't play games with sin—they put it to death.

This also means applying the gospel to our hearts, rather than simply resisting sin in our behaviour. We need to remember our obligation to the one who has given us spiritual life now and will give us perfect bodies in the future. Sin can only be cut off at the root if we expose ourselves constantly to the unimaginable love of Christ for us. Sin grows when we think we deserve something from God, or life. Godliness grows when we remember we are debtors to God, throughout life. Putting sin to death is part of what it means to have our "minds set on what the Spirit desires" (v 5).

☑ Apply

Write down a sin pattern you struggle with.

> ❷ *How can you put it to death? Think of a "mini-sermon" you can preach to yourself about Christ, and your debt to him.*

 Bible in a year: Jeremiah 46 – 47 • Zechariah 9 • Luke 10

Adopted heirs

These few short verses are a wonderful summary of the relationship you and I, as Christians, enjoy with God, by his Spirit.

Read Romans 8:14-17

Children of God

❷ *Who are "children of God" (v 14)?*

Verse 15 tells us that this sonship is a "received" status, not a natural one. We are not born as God's children; we are adopted into his family when we receive his Spirit.

In the Roman world, a wealthy, childless man might adopt someone as his heir. (This heir would be male, and so Paul describes all Christians—men and women—as "sons".) The moment adoption occurred...

- the new son's old debts were cancelled.
- he got a new name and became heir of all his new father had.
- his new father became liable for all his actions.
- the new son had an obligation to please and honour his father.

···· TIME OUT ···

❷ *Why is it amazing to have been adopted in this way by God?*

Privileged children

❷ *What are the privileges of being an adopted son of God?*
- *v 15a*   • *end of v 15*
- *v 16*   • *v 17*

In verse 15, Paul draws a distinction between two "Spirits"—two ways of thinking about and relating to God. The first is an attitude based on "fear"; the attitude of a slave. A slave obeys because he has to; he fears punishment and is insecure. It is the view that says, "I must perform well in my work for God, and then he will pay me my wages—he will answer my prayers, protect me and so on. But if I perform poorly, he might fire me."

But Paul says we did not receive this kind of relationship to God. "The Spirit you received brought about your adoption to sonship." The Spirit gives us the ability and confidence to approach God as Father, not as a slavemaster or boss. A child obeys out of love for his daddy; he knows the security of ongoing forgiveness and unconditional love. It is the view that says, "I am a child of God, and he loves me and will give me more than I deserve. My performance doesn't change my position in the family— but I want to work hard for him, because he's my loving Father."

⌃ Pray

One of the privileges of sonship is that the Spirit enables us to "cry, 'Abba, Father'". Abba means "Daddy".

Pray to God as your Father now. Enjoy this intimacy with him. And cry out to him for help in areas where you are struggling or sad.

Looking forward

This world, and each of us, are not what we were meant to be. But one day, we will be. This certainty is what Paul calls "hope".

Read Romans 8:18-25

Where nature's heading

❓ *What does Paul tell us about nature?*
- *v 20*   • *v 22*

The creation is in "bondage to decay" (v 21). It is caught in a continuous cycle of death and decomposition. Life always ends in death.

❓ *What does Paul tell us about nature's future (v 21)?*

❓ *When will this happen (v 19)?*

When the full glory of our status as God's children and heirs is revealed, we will bring nature with us. The glory that is coming will be so blindingly powerful that when it falls upon us, it will envelop the whole created order and glorify it along with us.

···· TIME OUT ·····································

Some people see the material world as inherently bad—we should withdraw from the world, and be suspicious of physical pleasures. Others see the material world as all there is, and inherently good—we should enjoy, and live for, creature comforts, physical pleasure and beauty.

❓ *How does the view of the created world in these verses differ from these views?*

❓ *What difference will a Christian view of the world make to how we treat it?*

Where we're heading

❓ *What does Paul tell us about believers?*
- *v 19*
- *v 21*
- *v 23*

We saw yesterday how wonderful it is to be Spirit-filled sons of God. Yet all this is only the "firstfruits", a foretaste of the incoming harvest that we will enjoy in the future. We will be completely, totally free from the effects of sin and death in our bodies and spirits.

❓ *How do we wait for this day (v 23, 25)?*

How the Spirit helps

Read Romans 8:26-27

❓ *As we wait, how does the Spirit help us?*

❓ *How does this encourage us when we suffer, and when we struggle to pray?*

When we are too weak to act like children of God, the Spirit helps us.

⌃ Pray

Are there issues in your life that you don't know how to pray for? Bring them before God now, trusting the Spirit to take your thoughts and emotions and to pray on your behalf. Ask for an eager patience about the new creation.

Confident Christianity

Christians can be confident people—but not in ourselves, or in our circumstances. In the last part of chapter eight, Paul shows us the way to deep, unshakeable confidence.

Where confidence is

Read Romans 8:28

- ❷ *What does Paul say "we know" (v 28)?*
- ❷ *What people is this answer true for, according to verse 28?*

Christians are not shocked by the tragedies and hardness of life—we don't expect things naturally to work for good. When something works out for good, it is all and only because of God's grace, working for us, his children, who love him. When something goes "wrong", we still know with absolute certainty that God is working good for us. This means we are positive about life, but we're not saccharine or unrealistic about it.

✔ Apply

- ❷ *How does verse 28 give us confidence in...*
  - *good times?*
  - *bad times?*
  - *times of failing?*
- ❷ *How do you particularly need to remember that verse 28 is true today?*
- ❷ *How could it cause you to rejoice over an aspect of your life that you would instinctively only grieve or grow anxious about?*

What good is

Read Romans 8:29-30

- ❷ *How do these verses lay out God's ultimate purpose in history?*
- ❷ *What do you think each word in verse 30 means?*
- ❷ *What is God working to "conform" (or shape us into) (v 29)? How does this tell us what our ultimate "good" (v 28) truly is?*

TIME OUT

- ❷ *Can you think of a hard time in your life when things went "wrong", but which, as you look back, you can see that God used to make you more like his Son?*

Verse 30 is breathtaking. God foreknew his people—before the beginning of time, he knew us in a relational, loving sense. He set our destination, planning for us to be with him in glory. Then, at a particular point in time he called us to have faith in him. As we believed, he justified us—declared and treated us as righteous and blameless. And one day, he will glorify us—make us perfect in body and soul. This lies ahead of us—but because it relies on God's action, not ours, it is so certain that Paul speaks of it in the past tense, as though it has already happened.

ᐱ Pray

Use each clause in each verse we've looked at to fuel your thanks to God for what he has done, is doing, and will do, for you.

Our Almighty Father

It is easy, unthinkingly, to view God as almighty but as unconcerned with our lives; or as intimate and very concerned, but too pocket-sized to be able to truly help.

This psalm teaches us to pray to God as the almighty Creator, who "spoke, and it came to be", and the one whose "eyes ... are on those who fear him".

Praise God…

Read Psalm 33:1-3

The first three verses encourage us to praise God. But the psalms are always calling us to praise God! The question is, what truths does this psalm reveal that should drive us to praise God?

… for his mighty word

Read Psalm 33:4-9

Astronomers estimate that there are 7 septillion(!) stars in the universe. Physicists tell us that there are more atoms in a single grain of sand than there are stars in the universe. And the Lord God made them all. Every atom of every grain of every planet and star of every galaxy in the cosmos bears his stamp of ownership. He created it all, and he did it through his powerful word.

❷ *What is a right response to our mighty Creator, according to these verses?*

Verse 6 pairs God's word with the "breath of his mouth". The word for breath is the same word as the Bible always uses for the Spirit. God's word and Spirit always work together. So Galatians 3:2 tells us that we receive the Spirit by believing the word—the gospel

message. We should never separate the work of the Spirit and the work of the word.

… for his unstoppable plans

Read Psalm 33:10-12

❷ *What encouragement do these verses give us in a frightening and chaotic world?*

❷ *How do verses 4-9 help to convince us that the plans and promises of God that we read in the Bible will be fulfilled?*

… for his watchful eye

Read Psalm 33:13-19

Verses 13-15 sound a bit "Big Brother" to us. Actually this is very different. God's eyes are not on us to catch us out. Look at v 18-19. God is watching us like a loving parent watching a young child splashing about in a swimming pool—his eye is on us to make sure we are okay, ready to help us if we get into trouble. In the light of that, the final verses encourage us to put our trust in him.

Read Psalm 33:20-22

◥ Apply

❷ *What promises of God's word do you want to praise him for today?*

❷ *How would it change your attitude to daily life if verses 10-19 really took root in your heart?*

If God is for us…

God is working for his children's good. He has foreknown, predestined, called and justified us, and will glorify us. "What, then, shall we say in response …?" (v 31)

Q+A

Read Romans 8:31-34

❓ *What are the four questions Paul asks here? (Put them in your own words.)*
- *v 31b*
- *v 32*
- *v 33*
- *v 34*

❓ *What are the answers to each of these?*

Notice that the answers depend on the truths of verses 28-30. If the God who has purposed our glory is all-powerful, why be afraid of any opposition? If the God who has purposed our glory has already given us his most precious possession—his own Son—why worry about our needs? If the God who has purposed our glory has declared us righteous, and if the Christ who lived perfectly and died sacrificially for us is standing before the Father on our behalf, why listen to anyone (including ourselves) who suggests we are guilty, or unforgiven?

⌄ Apply

❓ *Who is opposed to your Christian faith and lifestyle? How does verse 31 give you confidence?*

❓ *What do you find yourself worrying about? Do you ever worry you won't reach glory? How does verse 32 give you confidence?*

❓ *What causes you to feel that you are too guilty to be forgiven? How do verses 33-34 give you confidence?*

No separation

Read Romans 8:35-39

❓ *What final question does Paul ask (v 35a)?*

❓ *What is his answer (v 37-39)?*

All the other questions are really just other versions of this one. The only thing that we really need to fear, the only thing that could really harm us, is to be separated from the love of Christ. And Paul is saying, *Friend, have you been called? Have you found the gospel coming to your soul with power? Have you asked God to justify you? Then realise this—that would not and could not have happened unless the great God of heaven had set his love upon you in eternity before time, and is now unstoppably working out his plan to live with you for ever in his family.* God's love for us does not depend on our attitudes or actions—if it did, we couldn't be certain about life and the future. It rests entirely on his decision and plan. So nothing can separate us from it. We can live with overwhelming assurance.

⌃ Pray

Pray through your answers to the apply section. Then spend time thanking God that nothing—nothing—can separate you from his love.

God's merciful election

Chapters 9 – 11 are some of the most difficult, and controversial, in the entire Bible. Before we begin, ask God for understanding of his word and humility before his word.

Read Romans 9:1-5

> ❷ *How does Paul feel (v 2)?*

> ❷ *Why (v 3-4a)?*

God has done so much for Israel, his people (v 4-5). Yet most of Israel has not put their faith in Christ, and so are not saved. The message should be clearest to them—so why doesn't all Israel believe?

God chooses

Read Romans 9:6-13

> ❷ *What does v 6b-7a mean, do you think?*

Paul turns to two Old Testament examples. Abraham had two children, Ishmael and Isaac; only one was part of God's people (v 7-9). Rebekah (Isaac's wife) had twins, Esau and Jacob; only one was part of God's people (v 10-13). Here, we learn three things:

1. The only difference between Esau and Jacob was God's "purpose in election" (v 11). God chose Jacob, rather than Jacob choosing God.

2. That choice was made prior to birth, "before the twins were born" (v 11).

3. That choice wasn't based on performance—it was made before they had done anything, and not on the basis of any works they would do (v 11-12).

This is the doctrine of election. The only reason Jacob received God's promise—and the only reason anyone has saving faith—is because of God's gracious choice. So, the reason not all Israel is saved is because God has not chosen all Israel to be saved.

Is God just?

Read Romans 9:14-18

> ❷ *What objection does Paul raise (v 14)?*

> ❷ *What does salvation depend on (v 15-16)?*

Paul's point is that—as God told Moses—God is free to give mercy to whoever he chooses. Mercy can never be an obligation. No one deserves salvation, so God is entirely fair to give it to all, some, or none.

> ❷ *What did God say to Pharaoh (v 17)?*

Pharaoh is a helpful example of how God "hardens whom he wants to harden". In Exodus 4 – 14, God hardened Pharaoh's heart (11:9-10). Yet also, Pharaoh hardened his own heart (e.g. 8:15). Both are true—God hardened Pharaoh's self-hardened heart. It is what we saw in Romans 1:24—God gives people over to what they have chosen. His mercy is never deserved; his hardening is always deserved.

⌄ Apply

> ❷ *How does this passage make you more grateful that you are saved?*

> ❷ *Imagine someone says, "God is unfair to save some and not others". How could you use 9:16-18 to answer them?*

Is it unfair?

Here is a further objection to God's justice in election: if only those God chooses can have faith in him, why are people held responsible for not having faith (v 19)?

Read Romans 9:19-29

TIME OUT

❓ *Have you heard people make the objection of verse 19?*

❓ *Do you feel it yourself?*

In verses 20-21, Paul says that God made us, and therefore he has rights of ownership over us. In one sense, this would be a sufficient answer on its own to the question of "fairness". Who are we to answer back to God? We are so far below God that we have neither the wisdom nor the right to question our Creator. If you have time, read Job 38:1-41; 42:1-6.

❓ *What does God "show" in judging those on whom he has not had mercy (Romans 9:22)?*

❓ *What does God "make known", in his mercy and his judgment (v 23)?*

In other words, God's glory is seen in him having mercy on some and passing over others. This is the heart of the mystery—we cannot really understand it. Somehow, if God had undeserved mercy on all, or deservedly condemned all, we would not see his glory. The biggest question is: if God could save everyone, why doesn't he? Paul says that God's chosen course (to save some and leave others) will in the end be more fit to show forth God's glory than any other scheme we can imagine.

Further, while God is the author of our salvation, we are the authors of our damnation. The objects of wrath are "prepared for destruction"—but it doesn't say by whom. Romans 1:18-24 and Ephesians 2:1-3 show that they are prepared for destruction by themselves. Objects of mercy, on the other hand, are prepared for glory by God (end of Romans 8:23). Salvation, throughout the Old Testament, has always relied on God's undeserved mercy (9:24-29).

⌄ Apply

What difference does the doctrine of election make to us?

1. It prompts us to worship God. I cannot praise myself in any way for my salvation—I will praise God.

2. It makes us humble. It was not our perceptiveness, intelligence or wisdom that caused us to choose God; he chose us regardless of anything in us. There is nothing in us to be proud about.

3. It makes us hopeful in evangelism. Anyone, even the most unlikely, can be saved by God—so I'll share the gospel with everyone I can.

4. It makes us confident. God is in charge of everything, and he is committed to us, to bring us to glory.

❓ *Which of these is something you need to ask God to give you more of? How will you let the truth of election change you?*

Why Israel rejected God

Up until 9:29, Paul has attributed the unbelief of most Jews to God's sovereign purpose. But now he identifies a different reason for their rejection…

Read Romans 9:30 – 10:4

A contradiction?

Throughout history, the Gentiles "did not pursue righteousness" (9:30).

❓ *So how have they now obtained this right standing with God (v 30)?*

Israel, on the other hand, "pursued the law as a way of righteousness", yet they have "not attained [it]" (v 31).

❓ *Why not (v 32; 10:3)?*

The Bible is setting two truths alongside one another:

1. God is completely sovereign over all history, including salvation (9:1-29).

2. Every human is completely responsible for his or her behaviour (9:32 – 10:3).

Paul is showing us that God's sovereignty and human responsibility stand in relationship to each other as an antinomy—an apparent contradiction. One example of an antinomy is the fact that light sometimes behaves as particles and at other times as waves—we don't understand fully how that could be (it is an apparent contradiction of physics) but we expect to understand it in the future as we get more information.

What we can say from what God has chosen to reveal to us is that it is God's action alone that saves someone—and that people are lost because of their rejection of the gospel.

As the 20th-century pastor David Martyn Lloyd-Jones put it, "We are responsible for our rejection of the gospel, but we are not responsible for our acceptance of it".

🔼 Pray

Thank God for your righteousness. Every step of your journey to saving faith was under his sovereign control; thank him for that now.

The problem with zeal

❓ *What is unexpected about the fact that…*
  • *the Gentiles have come to be right with God (10:30)?*
  • *Israel has not (v 31)?*

❓ *What does Paul give Israel credit for in 10:2?*

❓ *So what is the problem (end v 2)?*

Zeal must be based on knowledge. Israel's zeal stopped them listening to the gospel; it prevented them from thinking things through.

🔽 Apply

❓ *How does verse 2 challenge you? Are you zealous for God? And if you are, is it a reflective zeal or a reactive zeal?*

❓ *How does verse 2 challenge the idea that, "It doesn't matter what you believe as long as you are sincere about your belief"?*

 Bible in a year: Ezekiel 10 – 12 • Revelation 10

What Moses teaches

To show that Israel were deliberately rejecting the gospel, rather than simply ignorant of it, Paul turns to Moses, through whom God gave his people his law.

What faith knows

Read Romans 10:5-8

❓ *In verse 5, Paul quotes Moses. What does Moses seem to be saying about how to be righteous?*

Then Paul quotes from Moses' words in Deuteronomy 30, and makes his own additions (in the brackets). To understand Paul's point in Romans 10, we need to **read Deuteronomy 30:1-14.**

Paul says that here Moses is talking about "the righteousness that is by faith" (Romans 10:6).

❓ *What does Paul say the attitude of faith does not say (v 6-7)?*

In other words, faith knows that we don't need to do anything to be righteous. You don't need to scale heaven (Christ has already come down from it), or deal with your own sins in death (Christ has already done that). Faith knows what Moses taught in Deuteronomy 30—that we stray from God and deserve curses and punishment (v 1-2); that God is the one who changes hearts, enables us to love him, and gives us life (v 6); and that this does not require the impossible from us (v 11-14), but simply requires our mouths and our hearts (v 14)...

Read Romans 10:9-17

❓ *What is all that is required to be saved (v 9)?*

What Paul tells us to do with our mouth and our heart are two ways of saying the same thing. Our mouths will profess what we believe in our hearts.

⌄ Apply

Reflect a moment on your own mouth and heart. Do you:
• confess that Jesus is Lord?
• believe God raised him from the dead?

❓ *If you do, how does verse 9 give you great assurance?*

❓ *If you do not, will you do so today?*

No excuse

Read Romans 10:18-21

Here is Paul's final case against Israel. First, they have heard the gospel (v 18). Second, they have understood the gospel (v 21)—unlike the Gentiles, who have found what they did not seek, Israel have disobeyed what they understood and claimed to desire. Israel are truly without excuse.

⌄ Apply

It would have been easy for Paul to make excuses for his own people's rejection.

❓ *Are there people close to you whose unbelief you tend to excuse, instead of sharing the message of Christ with them, and praying for them?*

God's olive tree

Salvation relies on God's election. Israel was responsible for its rejection of God's gospel. So did this mean that God had utterly, and finally, rejected his ancient people?

Rejection not total

Read Romans 11:1-10

"Did God reject his people?" (v 1)

> ❷ *How is Paul himself evidence that the answer is "no"?*

Verse 2 reminds us that there are two ways of talking about "God's people". There is the whole of Israel—and then there are those God "foreknew", the elect.

> ❷ *What happened in Elijah's time, when it seemed God was utterly rejected (v 2-5)?*

There will always be a faithful remnant within Israel, saved and preserved by God.

Verse 7 is a difficult verse. Remember that Israel sought a righteousness that they themselves could establish (10:3-4). So Paul is saying in 11:7 that Israel all sought righteousness, but when confronted with the choice of getting it through works or as a gift, the majority sought it through works, while the remnant received it by faith. And so the majority were hardened; as with Pharaoh, their hearts which were hard to God's grace were hardened by God.

Paul's hope for Israel

Read Romans 11:11-16

> ❷ *How is Paul hoping Israel will respond to Gentiles being saved by the gospel (v 11, 13-14)?*

> ❷ *What did the rejection of Israel ("loss") mean for the Gentiles (v 12)?*

"Envy" here is not negative. It is not (as it normally is) seeing what God has given to someone else, and wanting it for yourself, though God has not chosen to give it. It is seeing a blessing that God offers to all— salvation—and desiring it for yourself. So, just as the Gentiles could only have heard because Israel largely rejected Christ, so now the Jews can only believe because so many Gentiles have now accepted Christ.

Read Romans 11:17-24

Olive trees are cultivated or wild. Paul now pictures Jews and Gentiles as types of tree.

> ❷ *What has happened to the original branches? What about the wild shoots?*

⌄ Apply

Paul is "talking to you Gentiles" (v 13)—to us, if we are not Jewish.

> ❷ *How should what has happened to Jews make us feel, and not feel (v 20-21)?*

> ❷ *How do we prevent being "cut off" ourselves (v 22)?*

If we are chosen by God, we will keep believing and will not be cut off. But we show that God's sovereign love is on us by persevering—by remaining grafted into his people. **Read Hebrews 3:14.** Pray you will continue!

Taste and see

"Taste and see that the Lord *is good…" Really? Can we really promise this when we are talking with people about putting their trust in Jesus?*

We do need to be careful how we use this promise. It is not a promise of health, wealth and prosperity in this life, but it does express a confidence that God's dealings with us here and now are good enough that we should not be embarrassed to call people to put God to the test.

For once, we know what was happening in David's life when he wrote this psalm. You can read all about it in 1 Samuel 21:10-15. David was surrounded by people encouraging the Philistine king to kill him.

God is good

Read Psalm 34:1-10

As David looks back on God's rescue, his heart explodes with praise (v 1-2) and he calls others to join him in praise (v 3).

- ❷ *What was David's experience (v 4-6)?*
- ❷ *What can we learn from how God dealt with David (v 7-10)?*
- ❷ *What do the images in verses 7, 8 and 9 mean for us today?*

Fear and blessing

Read Psalm 34:11-22

Imagine this psalm as a church service. We've had songs of praise and testimony. Now we have a sermon.

- ❷ *What do verses 11-14 tell us to do if we want to be happy?*

To "fear the Lord" does not mean to live in abject terror. In essence, it means to treat God as God. He is holy, awesome and mighty. When godly people encountered him in the Bible, they found it overwhelming (e.g. Isaiah 6:1-7). It means that we should recognise that the God who tells us again and again not to be afraid of him is a God who needs to tell us that!

- ❷ *What motivation to entrust ourselves to God is given in Psalm 34:15-22?*

Read 1 Peter 3:10-12

Peter applies Psalm 34:12-16 to Christians who are not experiencing earthly protection, but are suffering persecution. Just as Jesus seemed to be let down by his Father as he died on the cross, so Christians will have times when we look at our lives and think that although we're obeying him, God is letting us down. But Jesus rose again, and one day we too will rise to new life in him. It's only from the perspective of life in God's eternal paradise kingdom that we'll really understand how good God is, and how well he treats those who trust in him.

⌃ Pray

Pray that you would be able to look back on how God has dealt with you in life and declare verse 8. Pray through verses 7-10, grounding your requests for today in the things God promises here.

The future of Israel

Israel's past is as God's people, to whom he made his promises and to whom he sent his Messiah, Jesus. But now they have rejected him. What does their future hold?

A glorious future

Read Romans 11:22-24

❷ *Given that God has saved "wild branches" (i.e. Gentiles), what can he certainly also do (v 24)?*

Read Romans 11:25-32

❷ *What is the "mystery" Paul now reveals (v 25-26a)?*

The beginning of v 26 is startling! Who is it speaking of, and what is it saying?

Who? Paul must mean ethnic Israel, all Jews, because this is how he uses the word "Israel" in verse 25. But "all Israel" probably does not mean every Jew without exception, but rather, the great mass of Jewish people (especially as in v 32 this is clearly the way Paul uses "all").

What? They will be saved—which, given Paul's Old Testament quotations in v 26-27, must mean they will have their sins taken away by a deliverer—by Jesus. Paul is saying that at some point Israel as a whole will experience salvation through Jesus Christ.

We are not told whether it will happen suddenly or gradually, but we will arrive at a point where more or most Jews have come to believe in Jesus.

⌄ Apply

❷ *Do you pray for the salvation of God's ancient people?*

❷ *Do you know Jews you could seek to share the gospel of the Messiah with?*

A glorious God

Read Romans 11:33-36

❷ *How are these verses different in tone to the previous three chapters?*

❷ *What does Paul praise God for?*

What do we learn from Paul's worship here?

1. *There should be no worship without truth.* Paul is quoting the Old Testament throughout these verses—Scripture must be the centre of all praise.

2. *There should be no study without worship.* Chapters 9 – 11 are dealing with complex, deep doctrines. Paul responds in praise. He uses truth to see and worship God.

3. *Doctrines that exalt God lead to the greatest joy.* The more we see our weak dependence, and God's sovereignty and mercy in election, the more we worship him.

4. *We don't need to understand everything to praise God.* Paul knows he cannot fully trace out God's ways (v 33), but he is not troubled by this. We should praise God for all we know of him, and not be deflected by what we don't understand.

⌃ Pray

Use verses 33-36 to praise God now. Why not begin your prayers for the rest of this month with these wonderful words?

The gospel-driven life

Chapter 12 begins, "Therefore". Paul is about to give a summary of the Christian life that should issue from everything he's said about the gospel so far.

Read Romans 12:1-2

I urge you...

❷ *What are we urged to do (v 1)?*

❷ *What do you think this means, practically?*

In speaking of sacrifice, Paul uses an image of a worshipper at the temple who comes in with an offering. Not a sin offering (an animal which shed blood for forgiveness)— Jesus is our sin offering. The offering Paul is pointing to is a whole burnt offering, which was where you brought a valuable, blemish-free animal from your flock. It was a way of showing that all you had was at God's disposal—that you were going to give God your best, not your leftovers.

❷ *What is the motivation for living this way (v 1)?*

❷ *From chapters 1 – 11, what have we seen "God's mercy" is?*

The word "spiritual" (ESV, 12:1) is better translated "logical". If you have a good view of what God has done for you, worshipping him with everything you have will seem sensible!

···· **TIME OUT** ···

Read Romans 3:21-26; 5:1-4; 7:24-25; 8:1-3; 8:14-17

❷ *How do these verses give you a view of God's mercy that motivates you to live sacrificially, out of glad gratitude?*

⬇ Apply

To be fully at God's disposal—to offer yourself as a living sacrifice—means...

• actively, to be willing to obey God in anything he says in any area of life.

• passively, to be willing to thank God for anything he sends in any area of life.

❷ *How are you currently living as a sacrifice, actively and passively?*

❷ *In what areas of your life do you need to offer God your best, in a way that costs?*

Do not be...

❷ *What should we not do (12:2)? And do?*

Conformity and transformation are not the same things. The first is to be shaped by what is around us. The second is to be changed internally, in a way that also changes us externally.

⬇ Apply

❷ *Are there ways you need to...*
  • *stop conforming to the outlook and expectation of the world?*
  • *pray for inner renewal and transformation?*

⬆ Pray

Thank God for his mercy. Use your answers to the apply sections to shape your prayers.

Thinking about gifting

Part of being renewed in our minds (v 2) is that we're able to see ourselves rightly, and see our place among God's people rightly.

Our view of self

Read Romans 12:3

❓ *How should we not think of ourselves?*

❓ *How should we think of ourselves?*

Our biggest danger when it comes to thinking of ourselves is not low self-esteem, but self-centredness and pride. So Paul tells us to be "sober"—not given to wild confidence or terrible despair like a drunkard, but being rigorously accurate. We're not to think too highly of ourselves; nor too little of our abilities.

⋯ TIME OUT ⋯⋯⋯⋯⋯⋯⋯⋯⋯⋯⋯⋯⋯⋯⋯⋯⋯

❓ *Do you naturally think too highly of yourself, or too little?*

"In accordance with the faith God has distributed to each of you" is a strange phrase. Paul probably means, *All of you have been given your saving faith in Christ, and that is how you are to measure yourself.* We are all humbled, and valued, by our knowledge that we are saved through faith alone. The gospel reminds us that we are equal...

Our view of gifts

... yet we are all different as well.

Read Romans 12:4-8

❓ *In what way are we distinct from one another as Christians (v 4-6a)?*

⋯ TIME OUT ⋯⋯⋯⋯⋯⋯⋯⋯⋯⋯⋯⋯⋯⋯⋯⋯⋯

How do you know what your gifts are?

1. Self-examination—take a sober look at yourself. What ministry do you enjoy doing? What problems do you notice and feel burdened by? What are you good at?

2. Ask others whether their opinion matches your attempt at "sober judgment"!

3. Get experience. In general, we don't learn our gifts before doing ministry—we learn them as we minister. So if you think you might be gifted in a certain way, work in that area and let experience guide you.

4. Study the biblical lists. Verses 6-8 list some of the spiritual gifts—others are in 1 Corinthians 12:28 and Ephesians 4:11. It is hard to discern your gifts without some categories to begin with—which is likely why Paul lists out gifts in these places.

⌄ Apply

Look through the gifts in Romans 12:6-8. (Prophecy here seems to mean preaching, or a message that conforms to Christian doctrine.)

❓ *Which ones might describe you?*

❓ *How are you using those gifts? How could you use them?*

Thank God for your faith and gifts. Ask for a right view of yourself, and for opportunities to discern and use those gifts to serve.

 Bible in a year: Ezekiel 29 – 32

Loving others

At the heart of the gospel is God's love for us. So at the heart of our lives should be love for him and for others. This short, packed passage shows us how to love others.

Loving Christians

Read Romans 12:9-16

"Sincere" (v 9) means unhypocritical—true to our heart. We are not to be polite, helpful and apparently warm to someone, while disliking them inside. A culture of "nice-ness" can develop within the church, where a veneer of pleasantness covers over a spirit of backbiting, gossip and pride.

❷ *Why does loving others mean hating what is evil (v 9), do you think?*

❷ *What happens when we think loving someone means never opposing them?*

Real love loves someone enough to be tough with them. If we're not willing to confront someone, we don't love them; we just love them liking us. Real love is prepared to do what is right, even if it risks losing some-one's friendship.

Paul could have said in verse 14, *Don't perse-cute those who persecute you.*

❷ *What does he say instead? How is this more challenging?*

Loving enemies

Read Romans 12:17-21

The end of verse 20 is an image of someone repenting.

❷ *What should we do (v 18, 20)?*

❷ *What should we not do (v 19)?*

All resentment and vengeance is taking on God's role as judge. But only he knows enough to judge rightly; and Jesus took the judgment of God. Paul is saying, *Either the person you are angry with will repent some day and Jesus will take their judgment; or they will not, and God will deal with it fairly. You are not involved in either process.*

⌄ Apply

Look at the list below and do a personal inventory. Ask yourself these questions:

❷ *In which two of these am I weakest?*

❷ *Where will I need them next (where will I next be tested)?*

❷ *What practical steps can I take to strengthen myself in these two areas?*

- Love people you don't naturally like with sincerity (v 9).
- Be willing to challenge evil (v 9).
- Love with dogged affection over the long haul, no matter what (v 10-12).
- Be generous with your home, money and time (v 13).
- Don't hold on to bitterness or resent-ment—instead, actively bless those who wrong you (v 14).
- Be willing to be emotionally involved with others (v 15).
- Be humble, willing to associate with peo-ple who are different from you (v 16).
- Seek peace in difficult relationships, and avoid revenge if wronged (v 18-21).

Christians and rulers

Now Paul moves on to the individual Christian's relationship to the state. This has daily, practical relevance for all of us!

Read Romans 13:1-7

❷ *What should every Christian do (v 1, 7)?*

❷ *What reasons does Paul give?*
- *v 1*
- *end v 3*
- *v 5 (two reasons)*

❷ *What has God established state authorities to do (v 4)?*

Many people obey the state because they don't want to be punished—except when there is no prospect of punishment. But a Christian is to be different—it is a matter not only of fear but of conscience.

···· **TIME OUT** ································

❷ *Can you think of examples from your life where you can disobey the state's laws without facing punishment?*

It is at these moments that we discover whether we are submitting through fear, or due to conscience.

⌄ Apply

❷ *Is there a way you need to stop disobeying and start submitting to the authorities God has established over you? How will you do this?*

···· **TIME OUT** ································

Read Daniel 3:1-18; Luke 20:20-25; Acts 5:27-33

❷ *How do these passages add to our understanding of how a Christian should relate to the state?*

···

In Romans 13, Paul says that the Christian is required to submit; and he was talking of very non-Christian governments. The default position of the Christian is to obey the government, even when those authorities disobey God's word. Christians are not to undermine a government which supports disobedience to God. But even in these verses, there are hints Paul is not giving an absolute rule—"the authorities are God's servants" (v 6). Obedience to authorities does not trump obedience to God. So it is right to courageously, yet respectfully, disobey and oppose civil authority when it requires disobedience to God—as Shadrach, Meshach and Abednego did (Daniel 3:1-18), and as the apostles did (Acts 5:27-33).

If the state supports what God forbids, we submit. If the state commands what God forbids, or forbids what God commands, then civil disobedience is a Christian duty.

⌃ Pray

Thank God for the authorities he has chosen to set over you. Pray that you would obey in every way, unless and until you need to disobey in order to obey God. Pray for Christians in countries who face these complex and costly decisions every day.

Nearer now than it was

Having detailed our relationship to other Christians, to our enemies, and to the state, Paul now turns to how we live within society, and how we live within history.

The only good debt

Read Romans 13:8-10

It is easy to interpret these verses very individualistically. But in verse 7, Paul talks about giving everyone what we owe, referring to taxes and honour. Verse 8 is also about paying what we owe everyone, yet now Paul has shifted to the whole body of our neighbours—all the citizens we live among. The Bible is clear that while God's people must not become like the world, they are to live in and contribute to the world, rather than withdrawing from it. Read Jeremiah 29:4-7, a message for God's people living in exile in a pagan city.

> ❷ *What are we to do, and why (Romans 13:8)?*
>
> ❷ *What does love not do (v 10)?*

In reality, we frequently don't see it this way. In the short run, it often seems that the loving thing to do is to break God's law, not keep it. For example, often we know that telling the truth will hurt someone, so we lie. But Paul says that we are not wiser than God; so keeping his law is always the loving thing to do. Usually, when we talk about doing the "loving thing", we mean "comfortable thing", for the other person and for us.

⌄ Apply

> ❷ *Are there ways in which you need to start doing what God knows is the loving thing, rather than what you think is the loving thing?*

The day that is coming

Read Romans 13:11-14

> ❷ *If we understand "the present time", what do we know is true (end v 11)?*
>
> ❷ *Because Paul remembers this fact, what does he urge us to do (end v 12)?*
>
> ❷ *What does this mean...*
> - *not doing (v 13)?*
> - *doing (v 14)?*

We must behave "as in the daytime". This takes imagination and reflection. We are to imagine that the day has dawned, that final salvation has come, that Jesus is right before us, and ask ourselves, *Now, how would I behave? What is really eternally important?* Or, to put it another way, *Since I am a Christian, legally clothed with Christ, how should I live in a way that reflects my clothing* (v 14)?

⌄ Apply

> ❷ *At what point today do you think you will live differently if you remember "the day is almost here"?*
>
> ❷ *Which desires of the sinful nature do you find it hardest not to think about? How could you think about the Lord Jesus Christ instead at that moment?*
>
> ❷ *How will salvation being a day nearer than yesterday excite you today?*

Bible in a year: Ezekiel 40 – 42 • 1 Corinthians 3

The saving God # 1

As God's anointed king, David was at the heart of God's promises to Israel—and so a threat to him represented a threat to God's promises.

Contend

Read Psalm 35:1-8

- ❷ *What is David asking for in these opening verses of the psalm?*
- ❷ *What is the relationship between David's description of his opponents and what he longs for them?*

As followers of Christ, we can only sing this psalm if we first hear it on the lips of Jesus. As God's promised King in the line of David, Jesus also faced people seeking his life and plotting his ruin.

And yet remarkably, Jesus called his friends to lay down their arms, willingly choosing not to be delivered from death, and so instead delivering us through that death.

Rejoice

Read Psalm 35:9-10

- ❷ *Are you surprised by verses 9-10? Why?*
- ❷ *What is the link between these verses and what's come before in verses 1-8?*
- ❷ *What do you make of David's confidence in the outcome he expects?*

This isn't simply about David getting even with his enemies. This is about God acting according to his promises and therefore being shown to be the God who saves. Although we're already forgiven, we too await our ultimate salvation on the day Jesus returns (e.g. Romans 5:9-10).

How long?

Read Psalm 35:11-16

- ❷ *What does David tell us about his treatment of those who caused his suffering (v 11-14)?*

···· TIME OUT ··

We probably all know the experience of treating someone with kindness, only for that to be thrown back in our face. Or maybe we've made a mistake, and someone's pounced with the stinging words, "And you call yourself a Christian?!"

Read Romans 12:17-21

As in David's example, Paul exhorts us to "not repay anyone evil for evil". Yet this doesn't mean justice is defunct and we're to pretend nothing's happened. Rather, it's precisely because we know that one day God will deliver justice (12:19) that we can go on blessing those who wrong us now, while also longing for that day to come soon.

✔ Apply

- ❷ *How often do you pray for that day when Jesus returns and our souls will delight in his salvation?*
- ❷ *What difference would it make today to know that day is coming?*
- ❷ *In what way do David's actions in Psalm 35:13-14 challenge your attitude to those who oppose you for following Jesus?*

Disputable judgment

Chapters 1 – 5 enable us to understand the gospel; chapters 6 – 8, to experience it;
chapters 12 – 13, to live it out lovingly. In chapter 14, Paul applies it to a specific issue.

Read Romans 14:1-23

The basic principle

❷ *What is the principle (v 1)?*

❷ *What "disputable matters" seem to have been causing problems within this congregation?*
  • *v 2-3*   • *v 5*   • *v 21*

A Christian "whose faith is weak" (v 1) is not someone who is struggling with doubts. It is someone who loses the focus of the gospel—that we are not accepted by God because we keep to a list of do's and dont's, but because we are in Christ. They may believe in Christ very strongly, and be fervent about pleasing him. But they are weaker in that they haven't applied the gospel of justification by grace alone to various areas of their life. A stronger Christian in this sense is simply one who knows that they are free to choose how to live and worship in particular areas—for instance, in drinking alcohol, or what style of music to use in church.

❷ *Why should stronger and weaker Christians not condemn each other?*
  • *end v 3-4*   • *v 9-10*

A word to the weak

Verse 3 reminds the "weak" that they will tend to judge—to condemn—the strong. They will tend to denounce the strong as doing things which are displeasing to God,

without pausing to consider whether this might be an area of life where Christians are free to live as they choose.

So Paul has two words for the "weak".

First... In Rome, the weaker Christians thought eating meat was wrong.

❷ *What does Paul say to that (v 14a)? What is he saying about the weak Christian's opinion?*

Paul is bluntly saying that their position is not biblical! When we are tempted to condemn another Christian as "wrong", we need to first ask, "What does the Bible say? Could it be that I am wrong, not them?"

❷ *Second... What are we not to be "passing judgment" about (v 13)?*

Weak Christians need to learn to distinguish between matters of principle (i.e. where God has expressly forbidden or commanded something) and matters of individual preference, or of broad disagreement between Christians. We need to ask, "Does the Bible give freedom on this issue? Could it be that I am making a disputable matter into an indisputable one?"

···· TIME OUT ··

❷ *What are the "disputable matters" among Christians in your church or culture, which see Christians condemning others (remember that not every matter is disputable!)?*

A word to the strong

We've seen Paul challenging the weak Christian; the stronger Christian's position is more biblical (v 14). But then he gives more criticism to the strong than the weak!

Read Romans 14:1-23

Remember, a "strong" Christian is one who has a grasp on the gospel—who knows that we are acceptable to God in Christ, not because we keep rules; and who understands the difference between matters of biblical command, and matters of conscience— "disputable matters" (v 1).

❓ *How does this Christian, who "eats everything", tend to look at their weaker brothers and sisters (v 3)?*

Since their practice is not forbidden by God, why should they stop doing it?! It's the weaker Christian's problem, not theirs— they are in the right, and are clearly wiser and more mature than the weaker Christians who have the issue.

❓ *But what is the stronger Christian's problem (v 15)?*

❓ *How is the end of verse 15 a stark warning to stronger Christians?*

If a strong Christian's behaviour leads a weak Christian to follow their example, against their conscience, then the weak Christian is sinning (v 23)—they prioritise fitting in, or their own enjoyment, over faithfulness to God. And they will feel guilty, and then ignore that guilt, and become open to doing other things that are truly wrong. So the stronger Christian, even though their actions are permitted, has "destroyed" the weaker Christian. And, Paul adds, Christ died for them (v 15). He treated

them with utmost care, and so must other Christians.

❓ *What point is Paul making in v 17-18? What should be the priority in how we choose to live as Christians?*

❓ *Why would verse 20 be a helpful corrective to a Christian who is tempted to continue behaving in a way another Christian finds wrong or troubling?*

Apply

❓ *Do you ever think about how your (right) behaviour might impact on other Christians?*

❓ *Are there things that you could, and should, stop doing, in order to help and encourage weaker believers? Are you willing to curb your freedom for the sake of others?*

❓ *Are there things you condemn other Christians for that are really matters of conscience, and disputable?*

Pray

It takes great wisdom to see where we are being weak and/or strong.

Pray that God would enable you to see any areas where you are being weak and condemnatory, or strong but acting as a stumbling block. Talk to the Lord about any specific ways Paul's words have challenged you.

 Bible in a year: Ezekiel 46 – 48 • Ephesians 5

A life of unity

In his final two chapters, Paul continues to apply the gospel to the church, focusing on unity and mission.

Living for others

Read Romans 15:1-4

❓ *What two principles does Paul lay down here?*   • *v 1*   • *v 2*

This is about our "neighbour" (v 2)—not only our Christian family, but everyone.

❓ *Whose example are we following when we live like this (v 3)?*

Paul makes this point with an Old Testament quotation, which leads him to make a brief, significant comment about the Bible.

❓ *Why was every part of the Scriptures written (v 4)?*

This means the Bible is: entirely applicable to today—every bit is designed for us, and has lessons and applications for us; it is centred on Christ (Paul quotes from Psalm 69 and applies it to Christ, because all the Scriptures are about him—see Luke 24:27); and hope-increasing—as we listen to the Bible, we find ourselves enduring in hard work and discipline, and encouraged by its precious promises.

···· TIME OUT ··

The sweeping principle for Christian living here is that wherever we have power (whether it is financial, or social, or in terms of popularity or confidence), we must use that power to build up and do good for those who do not have it.

❓ *How would this apply to our:*
  • *finances?*   • *church leadership?*
  • *relationships?* • *choice of where to live?*

⌄ Apply

❓ *How are you currently obeying Romans 15:2? How could you do so in new or increased ways?*

❓ *How will you use v 3 to motivate you?*

Living with others

Read Romans 15:5-13

❓ *What does Paul pray for this church will be given (v 5)?*

❓ *How do we live out this "unity" (v 7)?*

We learn here that real Christian unity...

• is a supernatural gift—no method can create it, we need God to give it.

• comes from discipleship—unity is a by-product of seeking something other than unity, i.e. following Christ (v 5). Unity doesn't come by seeking it directly.

• happens as we worship together—"one ... voice" (v 6) likely means corporate worship.

• is based on justification by Christ (v 7)— as we realise God accepts us despite our flaws, we accept others in the same way.

• is part of God's great plan—both Jews and Gentiles are brought together by the gospel to praise God (v 8-12).

A life on mission

Paul spent his life, and gave his life, sharing the gospel with thousands of people. Why? And how? And how can his example help us in our evangelism today?

Read Romans 15:14-24

❓ *What is the motive behind Paul's evangelism (v 16-17)?*

He describes evangelism as a "priestly duty" (v 16). The Old Testament duty of a priest was to offer sacrifices; so Paul is saying that his evangelism is part of the way he offers himself as a living sacrifice (see Romans 12:1). It is a way he can give God praise and thanks—an offering in response to all Jesus has given him.

❓ *What is the purpose of Paul's evangelism (15:18)?*

So Paul returns to where he started—his mission to call the Gentiles to "the obedience that comes from faith" (1:5). Paul is not looking for some kind of conversion experience, but for completely changed lives.

❓ *What is the means of Paul's evangelism (end 15:18)?*

We are not only to tell people the gospel but to embody it in our attitudes and relationships. We are to invite people to look into us deeply and see what a human life looks like when rearranged by the gospel.

···· **TIME OUT** ···

Paul mentions "the power of signs and wonders" (v 19) that accompanied his message. In 2 Corinthians 12:12, Paul comments that these are "the marks of a true apostle". So it appears that, while miracles can of course happen today, we should not expect (or demand) them. Our "works" will likely not be powerful miracles—they will be the amazing witness of changed, obedient lives.

··

Lastly, we see the strategy behind Paul's evangelism. He was a pioneer, preaching "where Christ was not known" (Romans 15:20). And he was urban—following Paul's journeys from Jerusalem to Illyricum (v 19) shows that he preached and planted in cities, and then moved on, leaving others to take the message to the surrounding areas.

☑ Apply

Paul had special gifts as an apostle-evangelist—the power of signs and miracles—that we don't share. And he had a particular calling—to pioneer urban church-planting—which we may or may not share. But we can still learn much from his example...

❓ *Are you motivated to share the gospel with people? Who will you try to share the gospel of Jesus with this week?*

❓ *When talking about Jesus, do you make it clear that conversion means a complete life change? If not, why do you think you leave it out?*

❓ *How are your works matching your words? Does anything need to change?*

To God be the glory

Paul now draws this wonderful letter to a close in a way that is practical, prayerful, personal and praise-filled.

Practical

Read Romans 15:25-29

Having spoken of his mission (what we could call "spiritual help", v 15-22), Paul now turns to talk about giving "social help" to other Christians. It is a duty (something that is owed, v 27)—but it should also be joyful (we should be "pleased to do it", v 27). How can this duty be done joyfully? By remembering that we have received spiritual blessings through the gospel, and so we please Christ by giving away material blessings (see 2 Corinthians 8:8-9). In this particular case, the Gentile churches were able to help materially those who had helped them spiritually—the Jerusalem churches from whom they'd heard the gospel (Romans 15:27).

Prayerful

Read Romans 15:30-33

❷ *How can the Roman church support Paul (v 30)?*

Personal

Read Romans 16:1-24

❷ *What does Paul commend various people for in verses 1-16?*

❷ *What do we learn about the life of the early church from this list?*

Praise-filled

Read Romans 16:25-27

❷ *What does Paul praise God for as he finishes his letter?*

❷ *Why is it fitting that this particular letter ends with this kind of praise?*

Apply

❷ *How are you, or how could you be...*
- *helping other Christians practically?*
- *praying for those who are working for the gospel in dangerous places?*
- *living like the people Paul mentions in the Roman church? (You could pick a couple of descriptions that strike and challenge you.)*
- *praising God continually for your faith in the gospel of Christ?*

This is the end of our time in the book of Romans. Spend a few moments now reflecting on the book as a whole.

❷ *What has particularly excited you?*

❷ *What has particularly challenged or changed you?*

❷ *What questions or issues do you need to keep thinking about?*

Pray

Praise and glorify God! You could use some verses from the letter that have especially resonated with you.

Bible in a year: Daniel 8 • Revelation 12 – 13 • 2 Thessalonians 2

JEREMIAH: Corrupt kings

Churches and nations are damaged when their leaders are in it for themselves rather than for the people. As we rejoin Jeremiah, we find him facing the same problem.

Unrighteous kings

Read Jeremiah 22:1-5

❷ *What should the king be doing (v 3)?*

❷ *What will happen if he obeys these commands (v 4)?*

❷ *What will happen if he doesn't (v 5)?*

Jeremiah then takes these principles and applies them to successive kings in Jerusalem during his lifetime.

Read Jeremiah 22:6-30 (or verses 13-19 if you're short of time)

❷ *How did the righteous king, Josiah live (v 15-16)?*

❷ *How have these kings fallen short of that (v 9, 13-14, 17)?*

When they were desperate or life was going badly, they wanted God's help, but when they felt secure, they wouldn't listen and just used their power for themselves (v 21). Could God say the same about you?

God's judgment on these kings is justified and complete. He will completely disown them (v 24). David's dynasty is over (v 30).

Righteous King

Read Jeremiah 23:1-8

❷ *What will God do to the unrighteous shepherds (meaning kings, v 1-2)?*

❷ *What will God do for his sheep (v 3-4)?*

❷ *What sort of king does he promise to give to his people (v 5-6)?*

And when this king comes, he will bring an end to the exile, bringing God's people back home to him (v 7-8).

The first shock here is that after saying the dynasty of David is finished (22:30), this future king will be a branch in David's family tree (23:5). That's why we find Jehoiachin's name in Jesus' ancestry in Matthew 1:12 (aka Jeconiah). The second shock is that this king won't just be a human descendant of David; he will be the Lord himself (Jeremiah 23:6).

☑ Apply

Read 1 Corinthians 1:30-31

Jesus has become "our righteousness": the king who both does what is right, and saves us by giving us his righteousness. He is the fulfilment of Jeremiah 23:3-8.

❷ *How do those verses help you appreciate the benefits of having Jesus as your Shepherd King?*

❷ *If you have any power or leadership role, what will it look like to be more like Jesus than like the kings of Jeremiah 22?*

▲ Pray

Praise Jesus that he is the king we need. Pray for the leaders of your church and nation, that they would follow his example.

The saving God # 2

As we turn to the second half of Psalm 35, we need to make sure we feel something of the anguish David felt as he faced this ordeal at the hands of his opposers.

Read Psalm 35:17-28

Obviously, this awful picture of assault and abuse is not an experience exclusive to Christians. Indeed, nor is it something that Christians are immune from ever being guilty of, rather than victims of.

But here, David is the victim—and David is God's chosen king. As such he pleads with God as one whom God has promised to uphold.

Re-read Psalm 35:17-21

❷ *What do verses 17-18 reveal about David's relationship with God?*

❷ *How would you describe David's tone?*

❷ *How would you feel if you were David in this situation?*

Reading David's words over 3,000 years later, perhaps we could be shocked at David's tone. And yet David's analysis of his opposers has a powerful frankness to it.

Re-read Psalm 35:22-25

❷ *What contrast does David make with "seeing" in verse 21 and in verse 22a?*

❷ *How does this reality drive David's prayer for vindication in verses 23-25?*

David's repeating identification of God as the "LORD"—the God who makes himself known personally—highlights once again that his pleas for God to act are not simply for his own sake. Ultimately, he longs for the God of salvation to be seen and glorified.

Re-read Psalm 35:26-28

For most of the song, David has been referring to those who are opposing him. Yet, as he closes, David introduces another group of people.

❷ *What do you notice about David's closing lines of the psalm?*

❷ *What message do you think David wants to give to his listeners by ending like this?*

Sometimes it can be hard to stand alongside those who are God's people. That's because standing alongside them will inevitably involve standing out from the crowd ourselves.

⌄ Apply

❷ *What would it look like for you to delight in the vindication of God's people in our current cultural climate?*

❷ *How can you make sure you are standing alongside those who are facing "gospel flak" in Christ's name? (This might be on a local level and a global level.)*

⌃ Pray

Spend some time praying this psalm for the worldwide church, trusting in the reality that God sees and has set a day when every knee shall bow to the exalted Jesus (see Philippians 2:9-11).

Problem prophets

Some preachers say God will judge sin; others say he's too loving to do that. Some say certain actions are sinful; others say God blesses them.

How can we know what God is really saying?

Jeremiah found the same problem: in his day there were lots of other prophets reassuring people that the way they lived was fine and that God would never judge them. In this chapter he reveals the difference between their words and God's words.

False dreams

Read Jeremiah 23:9-22

❓ *Where do the false prophets get their message from (v 16, 18)?*

❓ *What is wrong about the content of their message (v 17)?*

❓ *What is the effect of their message (v 14, 17)?*

❓ *What pictures does God use to describe their fate (v 12, 15, 19)?*

The message of these prophets endorses what people have decided to do anyway (v 17). They aren't sent by God, don't speak for God and haven't stood with God (v 21-22).

❓ *How should we respond to such people (v 16)?*

True words

Read Jeremiah 23:23-40 (or verses 23-32 if you're short of time)

❓ *What have the false prophets forgotten about God (v 23-24)?*

❓ *If God is this magnificent, how can the prophets expect to get away with their lies? How can the people expect to get away with their idolatry and sin?*

❓ *How are God's words different from the words of the false prophets (v 25-29)?*

Hearing God's true words is often not an easy or pleasant experience! They confront our errors and call us to change.

❓ *Who speaks words like this into your life?*

✔ Apply

Jeremiah gives us questions to ask of every preacher, prophet, writer and teacher who claims to speak for God, so we can tell the difference between God using a preacher for his glory, and a preacher using God for their glory:

- Does their message come from God's word or their own opinion?

- Does their message call sinners to repentance?

- Do they miss out themes of God's judgment and the seriousness of sin?

❓ *Who do you need to stop listening to?*

❓ *When you speak for God (in conversation, or more formal teaching), how do your words measure up? Are there ways in which you might be tempted to leave out or contradict things that God says in his word?*

 Bible in a year: Psalm 137 • Ezra 2 • Nehemiah 7 • Zechariah 4

After the disaster

Exile to Babylon dominated Jeremiah's ministry. He predicted it would come, preached as it happened, and pointed to what would come afterwards.

Good news for exiles

Jeremiah spoke this oracle after Nebuchadnezzar carried King Jehoiachin and lots of Jerusalem's treasure and leaders into exile in 597 BC, but spared the city and the temple (see 2 Kings 24). Maybe the judgment Jeremiah had threatened had happened and the wrong 'uns had been thrown out?

Read Jeremiah 24:1-10

- ❷ *Who are the good figs in God's eyes (v 1-5)?*
- ❷ *What does God promise to do for them (v 5-7)?*
- ❷ *Who are the bad figs (v 8)?*
- ❷ *What does God promise to do to them (v 9-10)?*

It's not that those sent away to exile are better people; it's that God graciously chooses to act for their good (v 5). His promises to them are wonderful—a new home and new hearts, a glimpse of the promises of the new covenant in 31:31-34 and the coming of Jesus and the Holy Spirit.

Good news for after the exile

Jeremiah spoke this oracle eight years earlier, in 605 BC, just as Nebuchadnezzar rose to power.

Read Jeremiah 25:1-14

- ❷ *Why will the exile happen (v 3, 4, 7, 8)?*
- ❷ *What will it be like (v 8-11)?*
- ❷ *How long will it last (v 11)?*
- ❷ *What will God do after that (v 12-14)?*

The generation who were sent away would never see their home again. Seventy years is a lifetime (Psalm 90:10): it's a long time, but also by God's grace a limited time. By God's grace there is hope: after being sent away, their children would be brought back home. God's judgment would turn from them to the nations—you can read more on this in Jeremiah 24:15-38.

⌄ Apply

These chapters are full of God's grace. Those who had rejected God will be counted by him as good. Those who had hard hearts will be given new hearts. Those who were sent away would be brought back home.

Read Romans 5:5

- ❷ *How do these chapters of Jeremiah help you when you feel sad about the state of the world, the church or your heart?*

⌃ Pray

Praise God for the invincibility of his grace. Turn the promises of Jeremiah 24:7 into prayers for yourself and those around you.

A history lesson

It is said that those who do not learn from history are doomed to repeat it. But often it isn't easy to know what is the right lesson to learn!

A prophet spared

Read Jeremiah 26:1-6

This seems to be a summary of Jeremiah's temple sermon from back in chapter 7.

- ❓ *What does God want the people to start doing?*
- ❓ *What will happen if they don't do this?*

Now we find out the reaction to that sermon.

Read Jeremiah 26:7-11

- ❓ *Why do the priests and prophets and people say that Jeremiah should be put to death?*

Jesus was also accused of speaking against the temple (Matthew 26:59-62). How will Jeremiah defend himself?

Read Jeremiah 26:12-16

- ❓ *What right has Jeremiah to speak these words (v 12, 15)?*
- ❓ *What effect does his defence have (v 16)?*

Popular opinion swings to Jeremiah's side. He also has some influential backers.

Read Jeremiah 26:17-19, 24

- ❓ *What historical example do these elders point to?*
- ❓ *What lesson do they say should be learned from it?*

They quote Micah 3:12, another time when a prophet spoke against the temple. Some might say that Micah was a false prophet because his warning never happened. But these elders learn the right lesson: the disaster never happened because King Hezekiah feared the Lord and sought his favour, so that God relented. So Jeremiah is spared (Jeremiah 26:24).

A prophet slain

Now we hear about another prophet, Uriah, who was just as faithful as Jeremiah, but was not protected in the same way.

Read Jeremiah 26:20-23

- ❓ *How was Uriah similar to Jeremiah?*
- ❓ *How did he meet a different fate?*

The editor of this book has clearly put these two accounts next to each other deliberately.

- ❓ *Why do you think the account of Uriah's murder is included here? What lesson are we meant to learn?*

Apply

Hezekiah spared the prophet Micah and sought the Lord; Jehoiakim killed the prophet Uriah and hardened his heart. Only one of these kings was spared the judgment that God had threatened through those prophets.

- ❓ *What lesson does the Holy Spirit want you to learn from Jeremiah 26?*

Sounds good ≠ is good

Psychologists talk of "confirmation bias"—we believe what we want to believe and what fits with what we already think. This is dangerous when it comes to God's word!

Making a yoke

The nations threatened by Babylon have sent their ambassadors to an international conference in Jerusalem. Jeremiah interrupts...

Read Jeremiah 27:1-15

❷ *What visual aid does God tell Jeremiah to make (v 2)?*

❷ *What message does this visual aid illustrate (v 3-7)?*

❷ *What will happen to nations that don't submit to Babylon's yoke (v 8-10)?*

❷ *What will happen to nations that do submit to Babylon's yoke (v 11)?*

❷ *Is the message for Judah's king any different (v 12-15)?*

"Submit to King Nebuchadnezzar" would have gone down in Jerusalem about as well as "Submit to President Putin" would today in Kyiv. It hurt people's feelings and sounded like defeatist treachery—but at that moment it was God's word. The message to the priests and people is the same too (read v 16-22 if you have time). Jeremiah's preaching sounded negative, lacking faith in God's power to save, urging God's holy people to submit to a pagan oppressor.

Breaking a yoke

In chapter 28 we meet one of the false prophets Jeremiah warned of in chapter 27.

Read Jeremiah 28:1-17

❷ *What is Hananiah's message (v 1-4)?*

❷ *What visual aid does he use to illustrate it (v 10-11)?*

❷ *How does Jeremiah respond to Hananiah (v 5-9)?*

That's what I want too, says Jeremiah, *but without repentance, it's just wishful thinking!*

❷ *How does the Lord respond to Hananiah (v 12-17)?*

✔ Apply

False prophets didn't end with Hananiah.

Read 2 Peter 2:1-3

False teachers today are still among God's people, still difficult to spot, and still both destructive and heading to destruction. It is easy just to listen to preachers and teachers who are positive, popular, talented and who say what we want to hear. But we need to listen to teachers who speak the Lord's words.

❷ *How would you tell if a church pastor or internet preacher is a false teacher?*

❷ *What can you do now to guard yourself against false teaching in the future?*

▲ Pray

Ask the Holy Spirit to guide you in the truth, and that you'd listen to God's truth even when it's not what you want to hear.

Life in exile

How can we serve God in a society that dismisses or despises our faith? How can we trust God when it seems he's been defeated? We're not the first generation to ask…

Read Jeremiah 29:1-3

> ❓ *Who does God say has carried them into exile (v 1)?*

After this happened in 597 BC, many would have felt let down by God, while others believed the prophets who said that God would bring them back straight away (dealt with in verses 15-32). Jeremiah writes to tell them God's perspective and instructions.

A present home

Read Jeremiah 29:4-9

> ❓ *Who does God say has really carried them into exile (v 4, 7)?*
>
> ❓ *What does God tell the exiles to do…*
> • *for themselves and their families (v 5-6)?*
> • *for the city of Babylon (v 7)?*

Israel may have been defeated, but not the Lord! He is still the real King, even in Babylon. They were residents there, and not just refugees. They should settle in for the long haul.

And they weren't just told to pray *in* Babylon but *for* Babylon! Psalm 122:6 urges us to pray for the peace of Jerusalem; now they were to pray for the peace of the enemy's capital city!

⮟ Apply

Read 1 Peter 2:11-12

Peter says that Christians are exiles, living in a society that dismisses our faith and often feeling like losers for following God. But his approach to life in exile is similar to Jeremiah's…

> ❓ *How does Peter tell us to live among the pagans?*
>
> ❓ *Think about your city (or town or village)…*
> • *How can you and your church seek its peace and prosperity?*
> • *How should you be praying for it?*

Not a permanent home

Read Jeremiah 29:10-14

> ❓ *What will God do after 70 years (v 10)?*
>
> ❓ *How does God reassure the exiles that he hasn't given up on them (v 11-14)?*

The exile is neither the end of God's plans for them nor the end of hope. Similarly, the society we live in will not be our home for ever.

> ❓ *How does this perspective help us to stand out as followers of Jesus?*

⮝ Pray

Pray for God's help in living as an exile here—neither withdrawing from society into our Christian bubble, nor blending in and forgetting whose we really are. Pray for God's blessing on the place where you live.

Reversed destiny

Jeremiah has uprooted and torn down (1:10), demolishing people's false hopes and complacency. But once exile has come, he can plant and build and bring true hope.

Read Jeremiah 30:1-3

Finally, some good news! This chapter features four reversals: Jeremiah quotes a prophecy of judgment and answers it with promises of salvation. If you ever lose hope for yourself, the church or the world, this is the chapter for you!

Terror to peace

Read Jeremiah 30:4-11

Verses 5-7a sound like chapters 1 – 25: threats of terror and invasion (see 4:19, 31).

❓ *How will God reverse this (30:7b-9)?*

❓ *What reasons does he give the people not to be afraid (v 10-11)?*

"I am against you" (21:13) will become "I am with you"!

Injury to health

Read Jeremiah 30:12-17

Verses 12-15 sound like chapters 1 – 25: pointing out Judah's life-threatening, self-inflicted injuries and diagnosing them as terminally ill (see 8:11, 22; 15:18).

❓ *How will God reverse this (30:16-17)?*

The wounded will be nursed back to health by God himself!

Ruin to restoration

Read Jeremiah 30:18-22

Jeremiah has prophesied about Jerusalem being ruined and deserted (e.g. 4:29; 9:19).

❓ *How will God reverse this (30:18-20)?*

"I have withdrawn ... my love ... from this people" (16:5) will become "I will be your God"!

Wrath to reconciliation

Read Jeremiah 30:23 – 31:1

Verses 23-24 repeat the threat of 23:19-20, that God's wrath will fall on those who despise him.

❓ *How will God reverse this (31:1)?*

"The LORD has rejected them" (6:30) will become "They will be my people"!

These reversals are bigger than just a return after the exile.

❓ *What do 30:9 and 21 tell us about the person who will make them happen?*

A descendant of David, one of their own, devoting himself to be close to his Father: this is Jesus! By joining us in facing terror, injury, ruin and wrath on the cross, he shares with us the peace, health, restoration and reconciliation of his resurrection.

⌃ Pray

Turn the promises of these chapters into prayers, putting your hope in Jesus, the King God has raised up for us to reverse our destiny.

Bible in a year: Zechariah 5 – 7 • Revelation 6

What are you looking at?

This short song packs a powerful, God-given punch. David wants to expose the folly of taking our eyes off God, and so stun us into reconfiguring the lenses of our hearts.

We often think of the psalms as being songs all about God. Yet this song bubbling up in David's heart has a rather different starting point.

The sin of the wicked

Read Psalm 36:1-4

❷ *What is it about the wicked that David draws our attention to (v 1)?*

❷ *What do you notice about the different consequences that come from this in verses 2-4?*

David paints a pretty grim picture of people who have become so disconnected from the reality of God that everything else about them has become distorted and corrupt. Notably, they don't even know themselves anymore.

The love of the Lord

Read Psalm 36:5-9

❷ *Imagine David singing these verses. How would he sound, do you think? What might his tone be?*

❷ *How does the imagery David uses add to the impact of his message?*

❷ *How does his perspective on God contrast with that of the wicked in v 1-2?*

It's a stunning burst of praise, highlighting that the Lord is wonderfully unlimited and delightfully unimprovable. He is perfect in love, righteousness and justice.

This greatness is "earthed" in his sustaining of humanity and the rest of creation (v 6), and not least in the fellowship and refuge he gives us through Jesus (v 7-8).

And while we're naturally caught up in David's praise, it's also powerful to see how different David's awestruck response is from that of those who have no awe of God "before their eyes" (v 1). It seems that the way to guard our hearts from pride and sin is to purposefully set before our hearts the heights and depths of God's perfections and so praise him.

Read Psalm 36:10-12

❷ *What impression do these final verses give you about how David understands his relationship with God?*

Apply

❷ *Upon what, or whom, is your gaze fixed at the moment?*

❷ *What would it look like for you to sing again of our boundless and beautiful God?*

Imagine God's saved people singing verses 5-9 around his throne in the new creation.

❷ *How does that spur you on to worship God and pray to him today?*

Restored people

Jeremiah has found much of his message painful. But now he hears words from God that are refreshing and pleasant (v 26). So today, come and be refreshed!

Jeremiah is still reversing his earlier announcements of judgment. He does it through alternating metaphors of God as husband, father and shepherd.

Loving husband

Read Jeremiah 31:2-6

Chapters 2 – 3 announced a divorce between the Lord and his unfaithful wife, Israel, who has been a prostitute (2:20).

❷ *What does God declare about his relationship to Israel now (31:3)?*

❷ *What is Israel called now (v 4)?*

❷ *How will God reverse her current situation (v 4-6)?*

The motivation for all this is in God, not in us. If he loved us in eternity before he made the world, even our sin won't stop him loving us now.

Read Jeremiah 31:15-17, 21-22

❷ *How will God reverse her current situation (v 15-17)?*

❷ *How will God's relationship with his wayward wife be healed (v 21-22)?*

Compassionate father

Read Jeremiah 31:7-9

Israel has been a disobedient son who lives in a way that disowns and disgraces his Father, God (3:4-5, 19-21). The north was the source of the invading army (1:14-15).

❷ *Who will come from the land of the north now (31:7-8)?*

❷ *What will motivate this (v 9)?*

Read Jeremiah 31:18-20

❷ *How will God's relationship with his disobedient son be healed?*

There is hope for Israel "not because of who they were, but because of whose they were" (Chris Wright). The same is true for us—as God's adopted children, our hope depends on his fatherly compassion for us.

Protective shepherd

Read Jeremiah 31:10-14

God's sheep have been scattered and butchered (12:3; 23:1).

❷ *How will God reverse their situation?*

☑ Apply

Read Jeremiah 31:23-26

❷ *How does God promise to restore his people (v 23-25)?*

No wonder these words were pleasant! Matthew 2:18 quotes Jeremiah 31:15 to show that these reversals happen through Jesus.

❷ *In what ways do you need refreshing and satisfying at the moment?*

❷ *How do the promises of this chapter do that for you today?*

Renewed covenant

God chose Abraham and his family to bring his blessing to the world. But both Israel and Judah betrayed him and went into exile. So has God's plan failed?

This passage shows us God still has a plan to bless the world through Israel. Three times the Lord declares, "The days are coming".

New purpose

Read Jeremiah 31:27-30

In chapter 1, God called Jeremiah first to uproot, tear down, destroy and overthrow, and promised to watch to see that his words of judgment would be fulfilled (1:10-12).

❓ *What new purpose will God have in his dealings with Israel (31:27-28)?*

❓ *How will this end the defeatism and excuses that people have made for their sin (v 29-30)?*

Compare verse 28 to God's call to Jeremiah in 1:10—they were about to enter a new phase in God's relationship with Israel.

New covenant

Read Jeremiah 31:31-37

Israel have not brought God's blessing to the nations because they have had their sin engraved on their hearts (17:1) and have not known God or his ways (4:22; 5:4-5).

❓ *In what ways will God's new covenant be better (31:33-34)?*

❓ *What will be the foundation of this new covenant (v 34c)?*

These promises sound too wonderful to be

true—but God's promises of redemption are as sure as his decrees of creation (v 35-37)! God the Creator is also God the Redeemer.

New Jerusalem

Read Jeremiah 31:38-40

❓ *Jerusalem has been demolished… how does God promise to reverse this?*

☑ Apply

Read Luke 22:19-20

❓ *What do Jesus' words here at the Last Supper tell us about the new covenant promised through Jeremiah?*

What blessings we have through this new covenant in Jesus' blood! God's law is written on our hearts by the Holy Spirit so that we want to obey him (2 Corinthians 3:6)— our incurable hearts are cured. We can all enjoy a personal relationship with God rather than just knowing about him. All this is based on the forgiveness bought for us by Jesus when he died (Hebrews 8:6-13; 9:15).

❓ *How has Jeremiah 31 reminded you of how wonderful Jesus is?*

⬈ Pray

Praise God for bringing us into this new covenant relationship with Jesus, and pray that he would extend his blessing to the world through you and your church.

Field of dreams

Sometimes we need to trust God's promises in the most unpromising of situations. And as the end draws near, God calls Jeremiah to put his money where his mouth is.

Purchase

This chapter happens in the months before the fall of Jerusalem, in 588-587 BC. The end is near.

Read Jeremiah 32:1-15

Zedekiah has heard Jeremiah's preaching so often he knows it off by heart: *This city is doomed and so are you* (v 3-5).

> ❓ *What does the Lord tell Jeremiah to do (v 6-7)?*
> ❓ *How does Jeremiah show his trust in God's word (v 8-14)?*
> ❓ *What promise does this point to (v 15)?*

Jeremiah is under arrest, his nation is invaded and his city is under siege—it's hardly a promising time to invest in real estate. He has no children to inherit it and he knows exile is coming—but Jeremiah has God's promise, and that's all he needs.

Prayer

Read Jeremiah 32:16-25

> ❓ *How does Jeremiah remember God's power...*
> • *in creating the world (v 17)?*
> • *in judging the world (v 18-19)?*
> • *in saving Israel (v 20-22)?*
> • *in judging Israel (v 23-24)?*

I know you are powerful, says Jeremiah, *but this sign of buying a field doesn't make sense!*

Promise

In verses 26-35 the Lord reiterates why he is judging Judah (read them if you have time).

Read Jeremiah 32:36-44

Again, the Lord reverses one of Jeremiah's own prophecies of judgment!

> ❓ *What will the Lord do for his people (v 36-38)?*
> ❓ *What will he do in his people (v 39-41)?*
> ❓ *Why is it worth buying that field (v 42-44)?*

God's people will worship him with undivided hearts (v 39) because God is determined to do good to them with an undivided heart (v 41). He's done this by sending his Son to the cross and his Spirit into our hearts. He will turn calamity into prosperity (v 42).

✅ Apply

> ❓ *What is there in your situation that makes the future look unpromising for you and/or God's people?*
> ❓ *Which of God's promises here do you need to particularly hold on to?*
> ❓ *How can you demonstrate today that you are trusting those promises?*

Use verses 17-23 to praise God. Turn the promises of verse 38-41 into prayers for yourself and your church.

Reversing the reversal

God has made wonderful promises through Jeremiah. In the final part of this Book of Consolation (chapters 30 – 33), he explains more of how they will come to pass.

The promises

Read Jeremiah 33:1-13

Seven times in chapters 30 – 33 God promised to "restore the fortunes" of Israel and Jerusalem (30:3, 18; 31:23; 32:44; 33:7, 11, 26). This phrase literally means God will "turn the turning"—to reverse the reversal.

❓ *How will God reverse...*
  • *the destruction of the city (v 1-9)?*
  • *the desertion of the towns (v 10-11)?*
  • *the desolation of the countryside (v 12-13)?*

Judgment will be followed by hope. These promises largely repeat what we have heard before in chapters 30 – 33, but now we are told how God will fulfil them.

The person

Read Jeremiah 33:14-18

❓ *What sort of person will God raise up (v 15-16)?*

❓ *Which two vacancies will be filled for ever (v 17-18)?*

Jesus is the only man who could ever truly say that his name is "The Lord Our Righteous Saviour".

Read Jeremiah 33:19-26

The Lord had promised David a family of kings and Levi a family of priests, but both were brought to a halt with the exile.

❓ *How does the Lord stress that these covenants are unbreakable?*

God's covenant is as firm and unending as creation. If the world still exists, then God's promise still stands! The Creator and the Covenant-Maker are one and the same God.

⌄ Apply

God's people need a King to rule and rescue them, and a priest to represent them before God and mediate for their sins (v 17-18).

Read Romans 1:1-4

❓ *How is Jesus the forever King we need?*

Read Hebrews 7:23-28

❓ *How is Jesus the forever priest we need?*

Look back through the promises God made in Jeremiah 30 – 33. All these depend on God giving us a king to sit on his throne and a priest to stand before him. Jesus reverses the reversal by bearing our judgment on the cross and giving us his future in his resurrection and ascension.

❓ *How have today's readings helped you to trust God's promises?*

⌃ Pray

Praise God for giving us Jesus as a forever King and forever priest. Ask him to continue to show you "great and unsearchable things" through his word (Jeremiah 33:3).

Promises, promises

We make lots of promises to God: baptism vows, lyrics in worship songs, resolutions after challenging sermons, bargains when we're desperate. But do we keep them?

Promise-breakers

After the bright vistas of chapters 30 – 33, the camera cuts back to the dark days during the siege of Jerusalem. It starts with a prophecy to Zedekiah about his, and the city's, fate (read 34:1-7 if you have time).

Read Jeremiah 34:8-22

❓ *What promise did Zedekiah and his officials make (v 8-10)?*

❓ *Did they keep their promise (v 11)?*

❓ *How did God expose their sin (v 12-16)?*

❓ *How will they pay the price (v 17-22)?*

They failed to free their slaves, so they will experience a very different type of "freedom" (v 17). One covenant ceremony was to walk between pieces of a dead animal as a way of saying, "If I break this promise, may I be like this corpse (v 18; compare Genesis 15:9-21). God will hold them to that promise.

Promise-keepers

Next, the camera cuts to a group famed for their faithfulness.

Read Jeremiah 35:1-19

Jehonadab son of Rekab lived about 200 years before Jeremiah (see 2 Kings 10).

❓ *Why did the Rekabites refuse Jeremiah's offer of wine (Jeremiah 35:1-11)?*

❓ *How were they an example of faithful obedience (v 12-14)?*

❓ *How were the people of Judah/Jerusalem the opposite of the Rekabites (v 14-16)?*

Both these episodes happen in the temple, and both include a leader giving a command to his people. But the recent promise is cynically broken, whereas the old promise is faithfully kept.

❓ *What is God's verdict on the promise-breakers (v 17)? What is his verdict on the promise-keepers (v 18-19)?*

☑ Apply

Read Matthew 21:28-32

❓ *How does Jesus' story show...*
  • *that actions matter more than words?*
  • *that how we finish matters more than how we start?*

Think back to some promises you have made to obey the Lord—at baptism or confirmation, or in church, or when praying or singing.

❓ *Are you more like the Rekabites or the Jerusalem officials?*

❓ *Are there any promises that you need to get back to keeping?*

⌃ Pray

Praise God for his faithfulness to his covenant promises, and pray that by his Spirit he would strengthen you to keep the good promises you have made.

Burning message

Here is the problem with the Bible: it doesn't say what we want it to say, and it tells us to do things we don't want to do. What will we do when this happens?

God's word written

We're back in 605 BC, the first year of Nebuchadnezzar's reign, when there was still time for Judah to repent.

Read Jeremiah 36:1-10

❷ *What does God tell Jeremiah to do (v 1-3)? What does Jeremiah tell Baruch to do (v 4-10)?*

What lengths God has to go to, to be heard in his own house! This scroll was probably most of chapters 1 – 25. Here is a window into how we got our Scriptures: God spoke words to prophets, who later wrote those messages down.

God's word feared

After the explosive premiere, the officials want their own showing.

Read Jeremiah 36:11-19

❷ *What do the officials tell Baruch to do (v 11-15)? How do they respond to God's word (v 16)?*

❷ *What do they do for the prophet and his scribe (v 17-19)?*

God's word not feared

Read Jeremiah 36:20-26

❷ *What does the king tell Jehudi to do (v 20-21)? How does he respond to God's word (v 22-25)?*

❷ *What does he try to do to the prophet and his scribe (v 26)?*

Jehoiakim's father Josiah discovered God's written word in the temple and obeyed it, fearing the Lord and tearing his clothes. Jehoiakim doesn't tear his clothes, but he does tear the scroll.

God's word rewritten

Read Jeremiah 36:27-32

❷ *What does God tell Jeremiah to do now (v 27-28)? How does God respond to Jehoiakim (v 29-31)?*

Fire consumed the scroll; now the fire of God's wrath would consume Jehoiakim and Jerusalem. God's word cannot be silenced— the re-release of these prophecies is still being read by us today!

⬇ Apply

When written down, God's word still speaks with his authority, and our response to his written word is our response to him—especially when he says things we would not have said.

❷ *How are you tempted to try to avoid or cut out the bits of the Bible you don't want to obey?*

❷ *How does this chapter help you to fear God and his written word? What difference will that make to your prayers and your life?*

A song of wisdom # 1

Songs are often written to pass on wisdom—think Cat Stevens' "Father & Son", Labi Siffre's "Something Inside So Strong" or, more comically, Baz Luhrmann's "Wear Sunscreen".

David begins by sitting us down, getting out his harp, and putting his lyrical finger on the matter of anxiety and envy.

Don't fret, do trust

Read Psalm 37:1-7

❓ *What reasons are we given not to be anxious about those who do wrong?*

❓ *Make a list of all the "positive" commands or exhortations given here.*

When we feel wronged about things not going our way, we might instinctively focus on the "cause" of our worry. In contrast, David suggests we spend more time proactively considering our own hearts. Instinctively, that's going to be more personally challenging! And yet we're told that as we "delight in the LORD", he will give us what we really need—and in fact that starts to become what we truly desire (v 4).

Refrain and turn

Read Psalm 37:8-11

❓ *What do you make of David's approach to seeing the wicked prosper?*

❓ *Is this different to how your culture encourages you to respond? How?*

❓ *What is it that gives David such a different perspective?*

If our gaze is fixed on the events of here and now, then when we're wronged we will be tempted to fear and perhaps even to lash out in anger. Yet David's words invite us to respond differently, knowing that a different reality awaits the world. Meekness isn't a characteristic we often talk about, or at least not positively. But Jesus did when he quoted this psalm—read Matthew 5:5. One Christian writer described it as being "amazed that God treats me as well as he does".

❓ *How does Psalm 37:1-11 help us grow in meekness?*

Better the little

Read Psalm 37:12-20

❓ *Note all the different ways that David describes the actions of the wicked and how the Lord will respond to them.*

❓ *What are the benefits of belonging to the Lord's people?*

⌄ Apply

❓ *What might it look like for you to take on board David's wisdom in your current situation?*

❓ *How can we help each other to "be still" rather than fret in such moments?*

A day is coming when justice will be done and God's people vindicated.

❓ *How is this a comfort in this world of suffering and injustice? How could you use this truth to comfort yourself today?*

The prison and the pit

Arrested, falsely accused, beaten, interrogated by a weak ruler, unjustly punished, but ultimately protected by God: Jesus was not the first servant of God to suffer like this.

The first trial

We've jumped forward again, to when Nebuchadnezzar is attacking Jerusalem. The king wants God's salvation, but not his direction (v 2-3). The Babylonian army withdraws, but only temporarily (v 5). Jeremiah urges the king to surrender in order to reduce their suffering, but is accused of being a traitor. Read 37:1-10 if you have time.

Read Jeremiah 37:11-21

❷ *Why was Jeremiah arrested (v 11-14)?*

❷ *What did the officials do to him (v 15-16)?*

❷ *What did the king ask him for (v 17)?*

❷ *What did Jeremiah ask the king for (v 18-21)?*

The second trial

Like Jesus, Jeremiah endures repeated trials.

Read Jeremiah 38:1-28

❷ *Why was Jeremiah arrested (v 1-5)?*

❷ *What did the officials do to him (v 6)?*

The prophet who praised God as a spring of living water (2:13) is now dying in a broken cistern. Like Joseph's brothers, the officials want Jeremiah dead without feeling like they killed him themselves. But an African brings hope...

❷ *How did Ebed-Melek help Jeremiah (38:7-13)?*

❷ *What did the king ask Jeremiah for (v 14-26)?*

✅ Apply

Consider Zedekiah. He won't obey Jeremiah but knows he speaks from God (37:17). He wants reassurance without repentance (v 2-3). He considers doing what God says but is afraid of what other people might do to him (38:18, 24-26). He protects God's prophet but won't follow him. He is an indecisive coward, and his fate is clear.

Compare Ebed-Melek (v 7-13). He isn't even Judean, but he courageously and publicly sides with Jeremiah the prophet. He gives Jeremiah practical and sympathetic help. He honours God's word, whatever the cost.

❷ *Can you think of examples of people you know who are like Zedekiah or Ebed-Melek?*

❷ *What would it look like today for you to courageously and publicly side with those who proclaim God's word?*

⌃ Pray

Praise the Lord Jesus that he publicly sided with you at the cross and went through worse sufferings than Jeremiah to save you. Pray that you would have the courage to publicly side with him.

 Bible in a year: Nehemiah 2 – 4 • 1 Timothy 6

The axe falls

The day of the exam, the day of the trial, the day of the funeral. You know it's coming, but it doesn't make it any easier when it does. So it is with the fall of Jerusalem…

In wrath

Read Jeremiah 39:1-10

The siege began in January 588 BC (v 1) and ended on 9th July 587 BC (v 2).

- ❓ *How did King Zedekiah react to the walls being broken through (v 3-4)?*
- ❓ *What happened to him and his family (v 5-7)?*
- ❓ *What happened to the people in the city, and the poor of the land (v 8-10)?*

Zedekiah's fate was just as Jeremiah had prophesied in 34:2-5. Having read Jeremiah 1 – 38, none of this is a surprise to us. We know this is God's judgment on Israel for their idolatry, injustice and immorality. God forgives those who repent, and he patiently delays judgment, but there comes a day when justice must be done. Yet God is not mentioned in these verses—is it almost as if he can't bear to look?

Remember mercy

After hearing about the fate of Zedekiah and the city, we now hear about the fate of two individuals who trusted and served the Lord.

Read Jeremiah 39:11-18

- ❓ *What did the Babylonians do with the prophet Jeremiah (v 11-14)?*
- ❓ *What was God's promise to Ebed-Melek (v 15-18)?*

- ❓ *Why does God promise to save him (v 18)?*

Ebed-Melek is the African official who interceded for Jeremiah to rescue him from the muddy cistern (38:7-13). Now we discover the source of his courage and compassion: he trusted in the Lord (39:18).

▾ Apply

Read Matthew 24:9-14

Jesus warns his followers that we will endure similar situations to Jeremiah and Ebed-Melek, when wickedness increases and the majority of people reject us and our message, and the love of most Christians grows cold. But as it was with Ebed-Melek, it is still true that "the one who stands firm to the end will be saved".

- ❓ *When do you need courage to side with God and his servants against popular opinion and powerful interests?*
- ❓ *When do you need compassion to help someone in trouble who others ignore or despise?*
- ❓ *How can your trust in the Lord Jesus help you in these situations?*

▴ Pray

Pray that the Holy Spirit will give you courage and compassion as you trust him, so that you can stand firm to the end and be saved.

Bible in a year: Nehemiah 5 – 6, 8 • 2 Timothy 3

False dawn

The city has been torn down; the weeds have been uprooted. Now Zedekiah and co. have been removed, might there be a chance for the planting and building to happen?

Gedaliah's rise

This chapter expands on Jeremiah's fate in 39:13-14.

Read Jeremiah 40:1-12

❓ *How did Nebuzaradan agree with Jeremiah's preaching (v 2-3)?*

❓ *How did Nebuzaradan show kindness and respect to Jeremiah (v 4-5)?*

The Babylonians appointed Gedaliah as their governor in Judah (v 7).

❓ *What promises did Gedaliah make to the people who remained (v 9-10)?*

❓ *What effect did this have on the Jews in neighbouring countries (v 11-12)?*

This was such a promising beginning: they were submitting to the Babylonians as Jeremiah said they must, they were being gathered together again, and they enjoyed God's blessing of an abundant harvest. Was this how the promises of hope after judgment were going to be kept?

Gedaliah's fall

Read Jeremiah 40:13 – 41:15

❓ *What warnings did Gedaliah ignore (40:13-16)?*

Just as Zedekiah ignored Jeremiah's warnings, so Gedaliah ignored Johanan's warnings. But Ishmael was of royal blood (41:1) and so had designs on the throne.

❓ *What crimes did Ishmael commit (41:1-10)?*

❓ *What effect did this have on the people left in the land (v 11-15)?*

It all unravels so quickly… The governor appointed by Babylon is killed (which will have consequences), civil war breaks out among God's people and greed and treachery reign. It reads like the end of Judges, where there was no king and God's people were spiralling into disaster. The promises of chapters 30 – 33 will have to wait for Jesus, the wise and godly leader whom death could not hold (Acts 2:24).

⌄ Apply

Ebed-Melek was godly, and God kept him safe. Gedaliah was godly, and was murdered. We see this mystery elsewhere in the Bible: for instance, James is put to death but Peter is miraculously rescued (Acts 12:1-17).

❓ *What is this telling us about the life of faith?*

❓ *How does this help you keep trusting God when promising beginnings turn out to be false dawns?*

⌃ Pray

Praise God that in Jesus we have a wise and godly King whose reign will never end. Pray that you would put your trust and hope in him when human leaders fail and setbacks come your way.

Bible in a year: Nehemiah 10 – 11 • Psalm 126 • Romans 7

Death on the Nile

Do you ever order clothes off the internet, but then send them back if you don't like them? You can't do that with God's word…

God's word requested

After Governor Gedaliah's murder, people were expecting reprisals from Babylon.

Read Jeremiah 41:16 – 42:6

- ❷ *Where are they heading to and why (41:16-18)?*
- ❷ *What do they ask Jeremiah for (42:1-4)?*
- ❷ *What do they promise (v 5-6)?*

Having been spared the long walk to Babylon, they now chose to trudge to Egypt. But halfway there someone seems to have said, "Hold on, shouldn't we just check what God says?" But they called him "the LORD *your* God"—did they want to listen to God, or did they just want God to confirm what they'd already chosen?

···· TIME OUT ··

- ❷ *Have you ever asked for God's guidance having already made up your mind what you want?*

God's word reported

Read Jeremiah 42:7-22

- ❷ *What did God say would happen…*
  - *if they stayed in the land (v 10-12)?*
  - *if they did not stay (v 13-22)?*

If they fled from the sword of Babylon, they would die by the sword. Often our problem with guidance is not that God's will isn't clear; it's that we don't like it.

God's word rejected

Read Jeremiah 43:1-13

- ❷ *What did they think of Jeremiah's message (v 1-3)?*
- ❷ *What did they do next (v 4-7)?*

They don't openly defy God's will; instead they claim to know better than Jeremiah what God's will is. They can't believe God would tell them to do the opposite of what they think is best. God had gathered them; now Johanan takes them away (v 5). Jeremiah had been freed by the Babylonians; now he is taken captive by Israelites (v 6).

- ❷ *What does God say will happen to them in Egypt (v 8-13)?*

This invasion happened in 568-567 BC.

⌄ Apply

How desperately we need the new covenant, and the heart-transforming work of the Holy Spirit!

Read Luke 6:46-49

- ❷ *Are there ways in which you treat God as a power to enlist rather than a Lord to obey?*
- ❷ *Are there areas in your life where Bible teachers and wise Christians have told you what God says, but you say you know better because you don't like it?*

Pray for grace to do what Jesus says!

Bible in a year: Mark 3, 5 • Matthew 9

Lessons not learned

Ever been on a trip which was spoiled by those you were with? The remnant in Judah have fled to Egypt, but they are going to regret taking Jeremiah with them...

None will escape

God's next message came once the remnant had settled in Egypt.

Read Jeremiah 44:1-14

❓ *What past example did God remind them of (v 1-6)?*

❓ *What anguished questions did God ask them (v 7-10)?*

❓ *What would happen to them (v 11-14)?*

It had happened before and it would happen again: idolatry + stubbornness = disaster. Yet it's remarkable that God still gave these idolaters another chance to turn back! There was still some mercy and hope (v 14). How would they respond?

Read Jeremiah 44:15-19

❓ *How did the men respond (v 15-18)?*

❓ *How did the women respond (v 19)?*

Same old message; same old response. Their interpretation was that the disasters hadn't happened because they worshipped idols too much, but because they'd worshipped them too little (v 18)!

❓ *Can you think of times when you or someone you know has blamed their troubles on following God too closely?*

In verses 20-30, Jeremiah repeated his message: there would be only one winner in the battle between their interpretation and God's (v 28).

You will escape

Baruch had stuck by Jeremiah as his scribe, but he hadn't found it easy. We now jump back to a message to him in Jerusalem in 605 BC—it's placed here to contrast his approach to God's word with Johanan's.

Read Jeremiah 45:1-5

❓ *How did the Lord...*
- *recognise Baruch's pain (v 3)?*
- *rebuke his ambition (v 4-5a)?*
- *rescue his life (v 5b)?*

Like the Lord's words to Jeremiah, these were more bracing than soothing! But the message worked—he was still with Jeremiah 25 years later in 43:6.

⌄ Apply

Baruch was told that his only ambition should be to follow God's word. Anything else was a bonus, as Jesus told Peter...

Read John 21:20-22

❓ *Do you ever compare your situation with those around you?*

❓ *Are you seeking great things for yourself? How can you focus on following Jesus instead?*

⌃ Pray

Pray that you will seek first the kingdom of God, and that the Spirit will help you to keep taking the next step of following Jesus.

 Bible in a year: Matthew 14 • Mark 8 • Matthew 18

A word for Egypt

God is the God of the whole world (not just of a few small communities of scattered exiles, or of a few small churches today)—so he has a message for the whole world.

Read Jeremiah 46:1

The Lord called Jeremiah to be a prophet to the nations (1:5, 10). Now we hear his messages to different nations, starting with Egypt and ending with Babylon. They follow the pattern we've heard before: uprooting and planting, tearing down and building, judgment and hope.

Judgment for Egypt

Read Jeremiah 46:2-12

The battle of Carchemish (605 BC) was a resounding victory for Nebuchadnezzar over Pharaoh. It came four years after Pharaoh's army had killed King Josiah of Judah.

❓ *How do verses 3-6 describe Egypt's power being defeated?*

❓ *How do verses 7-12 describe Egypt's pride being deflated?*

Read Jeremiah 46:13-24

Babylon's victory over Egypt will become an invasion.

❓ *Who will win this confrontation (v 15)?*

❓ *How will Egypt suffer a similar fate to Judah (v 19)?*

❓ *What pictures does Jeremiah use to describe Egypt's defeat (v 20-24)?*

The king of Egypt missed his opportunity (v 17), but there is a King who never misses his (v 18). God's people can have hope because our God rules all nations.

Hope for Egypt

Read Jeremiah 46:25-28

❓ *Who is God about to punish (v 25)?*

"Those who rely on Pharaoh" must include the group who took Jeremiah and ran away to Egypt to escape the Babylonians.

❓ *What hope is there for Egypt (v 26)?*

❓ *How does he hold out hope for "Jacob", meaning his people Israel (v 27-28)?*

Judgment on the invader means comfort for the invaded. The God who used Babylon to judge Israel and Egypt will in the future judge Babylon, and that will mean peace and security for Israel—and Egypt!

⌄ Apply

God still promises to judge those who oppress his people.

Read 2 Thessalonians 1:5-10

❓ *How is this promise of judgment a comfort to Christians who are persecuted for their faith?*

❓ *How can remembering that God is King of all nations help you not to be afraid?*

⌃ Pray

Praise God that he will ultimately bring justice. Pray for your persecuted brothers and sisters around the world, that they would not be afraid or lose hope.

Bible in a year: John 9, 11 • Matthew 20

A song of wisdom # 2

Great songs often tell a story. In this final half of Psalm 37, David weaves in the stories of two groups of people, hoping that we'll carry on listening in to his wisdom.

Read Psalm 37:21-40

Given famous verses like Romans 3:10 ("There is no one righteous..."), it might seem odd for this psalm to present such a stark difference between the wicked and the righteous. And yet we also know that Christians have been made righteous through our faith in the work of the Righteous One, Jesus Christ. Holding these truths together helps us see that we can humbly sing this song as we trust afresh in Jesus.

Making steps firm

❷ *What has David observed from watching the wicked and the righteous (v 21-26)?*

❷ *What aspect of God's character is David wanting to convince us of (v 21-26)?*

David seems to be intentionally presenting us with a tension. He is convinced that the righteous are never forsaken (v 25), and yet he acknowledges that often the wicked do prosper (v 21). Inevitably we'll also be able to think of examples of Christians whose circumstances have involved poverty and affliction. So does David's conviction (v 25) fit with reality? Let's see how the psalm develops...

Loving the just

❷ *How do verses 27-29 show us why David has composed this song?*

❷ *What reasons does David give to persuade us this will really happen?*

Never leaving them

❷ *What do we learn in verses 30-33 about what is driving the righteous person's life?*

❷ *How does this connect with verses 23-24, do you think?*

As David comes to a close, it becomes clear that he is not just contrasting the stories of two groups of people. He's also showing us that their stories are entwined. This is the messy reality of life this side of Jesus' return. So how can we endure?

Into the future

❷ *What point is David making in his observation in verses 35-36?*

❷ *Why do you think David makes the repetition he does in verses 37-38?*

Present circumstances are never a solid guarantee that things will go well in the future. Instead we're encouraged to see that only taking refuge in the Lord brings certain security.

⌃ Pray

Without this eternal perspective, the tension of blessing and opposition that Psalm 37 presents cannot be adequately or realistically resolved. Spend some time praising God for what awaits us. Pray for a life of "[hoping] in the LORD" (v 34), waiting patiently for the Lord's deliverance.

Weeping for Moab

Jeremiah has graphically portrayed God weeping over the sin and destruction of his people. Now we discover that his compassion goes far wider.

(Chapter 47 is God's message for the Philistines—read through it if you have time. There is no mention of hope for them here, but there is in Zechariah 9:6-7; Psalm 87:4.)

Moab's anguish

Read Jeremiah 48:1-30

The names in verses 1-5 and 18-25 are places in Moab, which was a neighbouring land to Israel. Chemosh was the god of Moab.

- ❓ *Why will the Moabites cry (v 1-9)?*
- ❓ *How helpful will Moab's god be on that day (v 13)?*
- ❓ *Who is really in charge of what happens to Moab (v 15)?*
- ❓ *What reasons does God give for sending Moab into exile (v 7, 26-27, 29-30)?*

Moab thought the mountainous terrain where she lived would keep her safe, but she became complacent, like wine gone off (v 11-12).

The Lord's anguish

Suddenly the tone changes...

Read Jeremiah 48:31-46

The eagle swooping over Moab (v 40) is Nebuchadnezzar, who defeated Moab in 582 BC after they rebelled against him.

- ❓ *How does God feel about Moab's destruction (v 31-39)?*

Wow! Moab worshipped an idol, defied the Lord, ridiculed Israel and plundered them when they were defeated—but God still weeps for Moab and laments over them when they are judged! Chris Wright gets this spot on: "It is not enough to affirm with Ezekiel that God takes no pleasure in the death of the wicked. We must also affirm with Jeremiah that God weeps over it."

Hope for Moab

Read Jeremiah 48:47

- ❓ *What hope does God hold out for Moab?*

"Restore the fortunes" is the same phrase God used 7 times of Israel in chapters 30 – 33, the one that means "reverse the reversal". God weeps over Moab's exile the same as he does over Israel, and he holds out the same hope to them too.

✔ Apply

Read Romans 5:6-8

- ❓ *How has God shown even more clearly that he loves the wicked and wants us to be saved?*
- ❓ *In the light of Jeremiah 48, do you need to change your view...*
  - • *of God and his judgment?*
  - • *of those who are currently rejecting God?*
- ❓ *And does your prayer life need to change? If so, how?*

Bible in a year: John 13, 16 – 17

Don't despair or presume

The Victorian bishop J.C. Ryle said of the thieves crucified with Jesus: "One was saved, that none might despair; yet only one, that none might presume".

The same could be said of the nations in Jeremiah's prophecy.

Judgment and hope

Read Jeremiah 49:1-6

❓ *What reasons does God give for judgment on the Ammonites (v 1, 4)?*

❓ *What hope is held out for them (v 6)?*

The Ammonites are offered hope "that none might despair".

Judgment and no hope

Read Jeremiah 49:7-22

❓ *What pictures does God use to describe Edom's judgment (v 9-11, 12, 19-20, 22)?*

❓ *What reasons does God give for judgment on Edom (v 12, 16)?*

The cleft in the rocks is probably Petra; Bozrah was a mountaintop fortress (v 16). When God comes to judge, there will be nowhere to run and nowhere to hide.

❓ *How does this message speak against the complacency of those who think that judgment and disaster can't reach them?*

If you have time, read the messages in v 23-33, which also have no mention of hope. However large these empires, however wise their experts, however rich their economies, however strong their defences, God will hold the nations accountable.

God holds out hope to most of the nations in chapters 46 – 51: but not all, "that none might presume".

Judgment and hope

Read Jeremiah 49:34-39

❓ *What will the Lord Almighty do to Elam (v 35-38)?*

❓ *What hope is held out to Elam (v 39)?*

⌄ Apply

Read Acts 2:1-12

When Jesus poured out his Spirit on his disciples to give them power to proclaim the gospel to all nations, Elamites were among those who heard God's praises in their own language (v 9). Jesus' death, resurrection and ascension restore the fortunes of the nations. Now is the time to spread that message around the world.

❓ *How are you already involved in God's mission to the nations (praying, giving, going, etc.)?*

❓ *Is there any way that God is calling or prompting you to be involved more?*

⌃ Pray

Pray that you would neither despair of God's grace, nor presume upon it. Pray for the spread of God's gospel to the nations of God's world.

Bible in a year: John 21 • 2 Peter 1 • 2 Corinthians 5

Even Babylon will fall

The empire of Babylon dominated Jeremiah's life and his prophecy. But even that world power is accountable to the Lord.

The oracle about Babylon is 110 verses long (compared to 121 verses for the other nations put together!). We'll look at the main themes, but do read it all if you can.

Judgment on Babylon

Read Jeremiah 50:1-3

Bel and Marduk were Babylonian gods.

> ❷ *What will happen to Babylon and her idols?*

Idols always fail, without fail. Babylon had been the nation from the north that would overwhelm Judah; now they will be attacked from the north (v 3—compare 1:14; 6:1).

Read Jeremiah 50:4-17

> ❷ *What reasons does the Lord give for judging Babylon (v 11, 16)?*
> ❷ *What is the standard that God uses to judge (v 16, see also v 29; 51:49, 56)?*

God will treat Babylon the way that Babylon treated the nations it oppressed. Jeremiah takes many of his oracles against Judah and repurposes them for Babylon. The bigger empires are, the harder they fall.

Hope for the world

Read Jeremiah 50:18-20, 33-34

> ❷ *What will Babylon's defeat mean for Israel and Judah (v 18-20)? What role will God fulfil for them (v 33-34)?*

Reversal for Babylon (defeat instead of victory) means reversal for Israel (rest instead of oppression). Even the northern kingdom of Israel will be restored along with Judah (v 19)! God the Redeemer will be defence counsel rather than prosecutor (v 34).

Read Jeremiah 51:59-64

> ❷ *How did these prophecies get to be read out in Babylon itself (v 59-62)?*
> ❷ *What sign accompanied the message (v 63-64)?*
> ❷ *How do you think these words would have encouraged the exiles in Babylon?*

⌄ Apply

In Revelation, Babylon stands as a symbol for all human empires that proudly reject God and oppress his people in their thirst for power and riches.

Read Revelation 18:1-3, 20

"The victory of God spells death for Babylon and life for the world." (Chris Wright). It did at the end of Judah's exile, and it will at the end of history.

> ❷ *How does God's victory over "Babylon" give comfort and hope to suffering and oppressed Christians today?*

∧ Pray

Join the saints in praying, "Amen. Come, Lord Jesus" (Revelation 22:20).

Judgment… and hope

We have read through 51 chapters of Jeremiah's prophecies. But how do we know they were, and are, from God?

Uprooted & torn down

Jeremiah's own words finished in 51:64. This chapter is mostly copied from 2 Kings 24 – 25 and is placed here to show how Jeremiah's message was vindicated.

Read Jeremiah 52:1-30

❷ *What happened to…*
- *the king they relied on (v 9-11)?*
- *the city they thought safe (v 12-14)?*
- *the temple they trusted in (v 13, 17-23)?*
- *the leaders they had confidence in (v 15-16, 24-27)?*

This is what Jeremiah said would happen if the people did not return to the Lord. His preaching exposed their complacency:

- They said they were God's bride—but Jeremiah said divorce was coming because they were unfaithful (chapters 2 – 6).
- They had God's presence in the temple—but they defiled it with their idolatry (chapters 7 – 10).
- They had God's covenant promises—but they had broken the covenant (chapters 11 – 17).
- They had God's priests—but the priests rejected God's word (chapters 18 – 20).
- They had God's chosen king—but their kings were unjust (chapters 21 – 23a).
- They had God's word through the prophets—but the prophets were liars (chapter 23b).

None of these privileges could save them without lifelong repentance.

❷ *How might churches and Christians today think our similar privileges magically keep us safe, however we live?*

❷ *What does Jeremiah's book say to any such complacency?*

Planted & rebuilt

Read Jeremiah 52:31-34

This is 561/560 BC. After reigning for 3 months, Jehoiachin spent 37 years in prison!

❷ *How were his fortunes restored?*

Here is a glimmer of hope from an unlikely quarter. It isn't much hope, but it is real Easter hope: a king in David's line is alive and freed and honoured. Jeremiah's threats of judgment have been fulfilled; his promises of salvation will be fulfilled too.

❷ *Which promises in Jeremiah do you need to hold on to at the moment?*

❷ *What one truth from our time in Jeremiah do you most want to remember?*

⌃ Pray

Pray that your privileges in Christ would make you faithful rather than complacent. Praise God that all his promises are "Yes" in Christ and ask him to keep you trusting those promises even through dark times.

COLOSSIANS: The hope

Peace. Provision. Forgiveness. These are basic human needs. Yet who could truly be relied upon to deliver them?

When Paul sat down to write to the Christians in the bustling town of Colossae, the Roman Empire claimed that it could deliver these things to its citizens. Paul knows that only God can give these things, and writes this small but powerful letter to make the issues clear for the believers there.

Hello

Read Colossians 1:1-2

❷ *How does Paul describe himself?*

❷ *How does he describe the Colossians?*

❷ *What ideas that are central to the gospel message does he include in his greeting?*

Grace and peace are not hollow platitudes; they are key to what sets Christ's cosmic rule apart from the rule of any human emperor or system. For who else can offer to every person on earth the wonders of God's undeserved forgiveness and mercy? Who else can restore us (and the entire creation) to everything we were created to be? This is real peace.

The gospel

Read Colossians 1:3-8

❷ *How did the Colossians become Christians? How did they first hear of the gospel?*

❷ *How does Paul describe the traits of the Christians in Colossae? Pick out the powerful phrases from these verses.*

❷ *How does he describe the gospel?*

❷ *What is curious about the order of faith ... love ... hope in verses 4-5?*

The logic of how Paul orders the so-called "Christian's trinity" of faith, love and hope is surprising. We might expect to find that love for others and hope of heaven derive from trusting Christ. But here, the linchpin for faith and love is in fact hope. A Christian's confidence gives them what they need to grow (v 7-8). God's promises in Christ are what makes the gospel news good: that is, because they are all about that grace we have been given in Christ. The Colossian Christians understood it (v 6) and knew it to be true. That is why they had a sure hope.

☑ Apply

This paragraph raises the obvious question of how someone might report on our own Christian walk.

❷ *What evidence is there that we are "saints" (v 2, ESV) or holy people?*

❷ *Think about your own conversion to Christ. How do you usually describe it? How might you describe it in the way that Paul does in verses 6-8?*

❷ *Genuine faith is never just believing things are true—that is, mere intellectual assent. What else is required to make it real?*

Bible in a year: Acts 16 • Philippians 1, 3

How to grow in faith

If you want to discover a person's real priorities, ask two questions: what do you spend most money on, and what do you most often pray for yourself and others?

A new commitment

Read Colossians 1:9-10

❷ *What does Paul pray for in verse 9?*

❷ *Notice that he prays for this continuously. Why is this so important?*

❷ *What else does he pray for (v 10-12)?*

❷ *How is this different from the kinds of things we often pray for ourselves, in church or in prayer groups?*

Ministry can never be simply about converts completing response cards at an event—it is about making and supporting lifelong disciples. The need to be filled with the knowledge of God's will is constant, and it is the most important thing—because it is from this knowledge of God that genuine God-honouring living springs, so that we might live fruitful lives. Memorising swathes of theology serves little purpose if it stays as head knowledge. The grandest purpose of theological knowledge must be to pursue godly wisdom.

☑ Apply

❷ *If somebody had access to your bank statements and prayer lists, what would they conclude? Who or what is the focus of your life from this evidence?*

❷ *How might you change what you pray for in light of Paul's prayer here?*

God's power

Read Colossians 1:11-14

❷ *What else does Paul pray for?*

❷ *What does this prayer suggest about the Colossians' circumstances?*

❷ *How do the statements in verses 13-14 form the basis of Christian growth?*

Paul wants every Christian to endure to the end. It means keeping going in faith, love and hope until the thing we hope for has been attained. But that is an intimidating thought—especially if the battle with temptation or opposition rages fiercely. The good news is that we are never abandoned to fight this battle alone. Just as the Spirit fills us with wisdom and understanding, so he enables the very perseverance he calls us to. In fact, the most powerful evidence for his invisible work must surely be the fact that believers *still believe* despite their horrendous circumstances. And that they are able to walk through their circumstances with a joy and a thankfulness that is supernatural.

And central to all of this is understanding what God has done for us in the gospel, and how we are now completely different. We may live in India, Britain, Australia or America, but we have a different and more permanent address: the kingdom of his beloved Son, Jesus.

❷ *What will you pray now for yourself, and for others?*

 Bible in a year: Acts 17 • 1 Thessalonians 1 – 2

He did it all for us

Sometimes a song will wrench our hearts, opening our eyes to all that a person has been through.

Just like Adele or Johnny Cash with some of their greatest songs, David gives us a song that pounds with a heavy ache.

Read Psalm 38:1-8

❓ *What can we tell about David's situation from his opening?*

❓ *What does David see as God's work in this situation and how does he respond?*

Initially this psalm might confuse us. David seems to speak of his own sin as leading to his physical affliction, as well as his suffering being a result of others' wickedness. How do we read this as Christians today? **Read Hebrews 12:5-7.** Christians can be confident that the punishment our sins deserved has already been wholly taken by Jesus on the cross. And yet, like any loving parent, God still disciplines his children as part of his great plan for our Christ-likeness. In fact, that's what God's doing all the time! It is not that we are being punished, or that going through a trial shows that we are worse Christians than others who don't face that trial. But it is that God is always lovingly bringing us into circumstances that will help us turn from sin and become more like Jesus.

Read Psalm 38:9-15

❓ *How are those close to David responding to his suffering?*

❓ *What do you make of the contrasts in verses 12-15 between David, his opponents and God?*

There are few feelings in the world like betrayal. And yet in the midst of this David knows he's not been abandoned by God. God even hears his sighs (v 9).

Read Psalm 38:16-22

❓ *How do these verses help us see how David understands both his relationship with God and with others?*

Strikingly, this could have been Jesus' own song from the cross. Abandoned by friends and failing in strength, he would then face the wrath of the Father for our sin. Although he cried out for an answer (e.g. Matthew 27:46), ultimately it was his willingness to be forsaken on our behalf that means we have the assurance that our own cries for a Saviour (Psalm 38:22) are heard.

🔼 Pray

Reflect upon how Jesus effectively "sang" this song for us, so that even when our situations may resemble David's, there is still hope and the Christian need never despair.

Spend some time entrusting your situation, and the situations of friends and family, to the one who knows all our aches and longings.

Image of God

This letter is scandalous. Its categorical statements about Jesus' uniqueness put Christians on a collision course with Rome back then, and with our modern world now.

Everything!

Read Colossians 1:15-20

❷ *Pick out the universal statements here about Jesus. How many times is the word "all" or "everything" used?*

❷ *What is Jesus <u>not</u> Lord over, according to these verses?*

❷ *What did he achieve when he died on the cross (v 20)?*

Jews would never have struggled to believe that there is only one God and that he created everything that exists. But for the many in Colossae from a pagan background, the idea would have been palpably absurd. They followed many gods and had many myths about the world's origins. But the idea that this unique Creator actually spent time on earth would have baffled both groups. Yet that is precisely what Paul insists had happened just a few years before. The man Jesus is Lord of *everything*. And the picture Paul builds for us is staggering in its scope.

He is...

Father: If you want to know what God is like, you need to look at his Son—because he is God's true image. Or, in the words of Hebrews, he is "the exact representation of his [God's] being" (Hebrews 1:3). Like a great portrait, Jesus offers a true likeness of the Father. When we look at Jesus, we see God.

Creator: Paul writes, "For in him all things were created," (Colossians 1:16). It is a staggering claim. If a great artist paints a masterpiece, he or she has full ownership rights over it, right up until the moment it is sold to a collector or given to a friend. Well, Jesus has never done that with his masterpiece. He never would. He made everything. So he owns everything.

Sustainer: Gravity may well exert the most extraordinary forces on everything from insects to planets, yet Jesus Christ, fully God and fully man, is the one on whom it depends second by second. As Paul says, "In him all things hold together" (v 17).

In view of this condensed catalogue of Jesus' qualities, it is no wonder that he has all the rights due to the "firstborn over all creation" (v 15).

☑ Apply

❷ *Why would people find the statements in this passage so outrageous? What might you say in response to someone who thought these claims ridiculous?*

❷ *Jesus is the image of the invisible God: how would you explain to someone what Christians believe about Jesus and his divinity?*

❷ *Jesus is the sustainer: how should this knowledge change the way we view both Jesus and the universe we live in?*

Mine!

"There is not a square inch in the whole domain of our human existence over which Christ, who is sovereign over all, does not cry, 'Mine!'" said Abraham Kuyper.

Yet this truth also raises a problem: if it is all his, why doesn't he do something about everything that has gone so badly wrong?

Rescued...

Read Colossians 1:15-20

❷ *Why was Jesus born?*

❷ *Why did Jesus die?*

❷ *Why did Jesus rise again?*

❷ *Why do we need rescuing? What do the verbs in verse 20 suggest?*

Ever since Genesis 3, there has been a simple root cause of all that is wrong in the world—from the grand scale of empires and nations right down to the personal level of playground bullies and marital conflict. It is sin. This is the human heart-attitude that consistently chooses to go it alone. It is a matter of creatures declaring independence from the Creator. We insist that we don't need God or his ways in our lives. Everything needs to be done our own way. That is treason of a cosmic order. We need reconciling because we are estranged from God. We need Jesus to make peace for us because we are at war with God.

... by his blood

Read Colossians 1:20 again

❷ *How is the truth of this verse under attack today?*

❷ *How does Jesus' death on the cross make peace? What do people still find offensive about that claim?*

The ancient Greek mindset took a highly negative view of all things physical and bodily. For a culture that prized the more "spiritual" realm of ideas and the mind, the body seemed to let the side down. But that is not God's style. He created the body and so is entirely pleased to embrace the reality of having a body. Bodies cannot be so bad after all, it seems. God's purpose in the Son becoming fully human goes far beyond simply proving that, however. He was pleased for this precisely because he was pleased to rescue his creation. And becoming human was fundamental to achieving that.

Result

❷ *What is Jesus' relationship with his people—the church (v 18)?*

The extraordinary thing is that the evidence of God's work of new creation is the existence of the church. God's evidence includes the church that meets down your street; and the fellowship nearby that gets up to some slightly wacky activities that you don't fully understand or accept; plus the tiny group of brothers and sisters forced to meet in secret because of an oppressive government regime. All of these are expressions of God's people living out their faith. As such, all are evidence that God is bringing about a new creation.

Radical conversion

Christians are people with a past, a present and a future. And in order to serve Jesus, live well, and grow to maturity, we need to understand all three of these realities.

Past

Read Colossians 1:21

❓ *What were we once?*

❓ *Does this description resonate with your own experience? Why/why not?*

It's a devastating diagnosis: alienated from God. We were hostile in our minds. Our thinking was opposed to seeing things the way God sees things. And we were doing evil deeds. You may have grown up respectable and well-behaved; you may have been part of a Christian family, and never remember a time when Jesus was not real to you; but you know the truth of these verses. On the outside we can look moral and "good", but we know that all our righteousness is like filthy rags.

Present

Read Colossians 1:22

❓ *What has Jesus done for us?*

❓ *How did he do it?*

❓ *For what purpose did he do it?*

Reconciliation is one of the most beautiful concepts in human experience, but it is also complex. It speaks of the joy of friendship but also the pain of relationship breakdown. Reconciliation can only come about if both sides agree to it, and it always requires humility. It requires the readiness to deal with the causes of that breakdown and the desire to rebuild. In short, reconciliation is hard.

And for cosmic rebellion, reconciliation required sacrifice, blood, death—the cross. The curious expression "his body of flesh" (ESV) or "Christ's physical body" (NIV) underlines that this reconciliation demanded both the incarnation and the real suffering and death of Christ to break open a way back to God for the whole of humanity. Our current status is that we are reconciled to God.

Future

Read Colossians 1:22-23

❓ *What three things does Jesus give to those who are reconciled to him (v 22)?*

❓ *How does this reconciliation happen in practical terms (v 23)?*

❓ *What is required of us (v 23)?*

It might seem that these "conditions" placed the responsibility back on us. But Paul's argument here is not about our efforts but about our dependence. Our faith is both established and firm. But it is ground that we must not shift from. Jesus is the one who has done it all, so it is madness to move away from him and to put our trust in other things—a theme we will return to in Colossians 2.

⌃ Pray

Thank God that you have been rescued from your past and have a glorious future that is secure. Pray that you would continue to trust him in the here and now.

The secret disclosed

We all love a mystery. Something inexplicable happens, and our minds are drawn to try and work out what happened, whodunit, what the solution is.

For thousands of years the gospel was a mystery. There were hints and rumours. There were suggestions and shadows. God forgave his people, and yet how could the blood of an animal atone for the sins of a human? It was a mystery. What were God's plans for the world outside of Israel? Were these non-Jewish people just all to be discarded? It was a mystery.

Revealed

Read Colossians 1:24-27

- ❓ *What was the commission given to Paul (v 25)?*
- ❓ *Who has God chosen to reveal the "mystery" to?*
- ❓ *What is the mystery (v 27)?*
- ❓ *Why is this mystery so shocking to the Jews?*

What Paul offers at the end of this paragraph is a summary of this treasure more succinct than any tweet and more momentous than any sound bite. For he summarises the privilege of being a Christian in its entirety in just seven words: "Christ in you, the hope of glory". The "you" here refers specifically to Gentile Christians.

God no longer lives in the Jerusalem Temple—which excluded Gentiles, the vast majority of people who live in the world—but he has taken up residence in anyone who hears the gospel message and responds.

Christ living within us is the foundation of our confidence. He makes the difference between worldly hope and Christian hope. Worldly hope is wishful thinking—of the sort that hopes for an Aston Martin or an all-expenses-paid tropical holiday at Christmas. It might happen, but it is very unlikely.

Christian hope is light years from that—it is full of confidence. Why? Because it does not depend on "me" in the slightest. It is only because of Christ. How else could I expect to enter God's glorious presence? I need the glorious riches of his revealed gospel. Only Christ can get me there. So I can truly say that he will get me there—because he promises to take us all the way.

⌄ Apply

- ❓ *"Christ in you, the hope of glory." What excites you about this summary of the gospel message and the benefit from it?*
- ❓ *What enabled Paul to persevere and even rejoice in his suffering (v 24)? Why do we find it difficult to feel the same way?*

Turn your answers into both prayer and praise.

How to be a servant

Wanted: Men and women of any age, background or experience to share the greatest news in the world. Hard work. Imprisonment and suffering probable. Death certain.

It's not a great job advert. And yet that was the reality of becoming a Christian in Paul's day. And it's also the same reality in many parts of the world in our day as well.

The gospel

Read Colossians 1:28

> ❷ Who is at the heart of the gospel message?
>
> ❷ How should we present this message to others and to each other?
>
> ❷ What do you think "admonishing" and "teaching ... with all wisdom" mean?

Admonishing literally means "straightening out". Of course, such correction should never be done in a spirit of pride because none of us can ever grasp Christ fully. We all need others to help us keep on the straight and narrow—both in our thinking and understanding and in how we live.

Teaching about God is a tall order! This is why Paul maintains that he does this with "all wisdom". He is not referring to human wisdom or worldly wisdom. This wisdom can only be a work of God.

As Paul prayed for the Colossians back in 1:9, there is a continuous need for filling "with the knowledge of his will through all the wisdom and understanding that the Spirit gives". But the impact on the hearers ultimately rests with God—it is his Spirit that brings wisdom and understanding, as eyes are opened and hearts softened.

Apply

> ❷ Do you talk about Jesus? Or about something else—philosophy, church, "God" in a vague kind of way? How can you help yourself to focus on Jesus more?
>
> ❷ Think about how you could humbly and carefully rebuke another believer about their thinking or behaviour. Why do we find this difficult to do?
>
> ❷ Pray that those who teach and lead in your church would do so with godly wisdom and insight.

The cost

Read Colossians 1:28-29

> ❷ What is the ultimate aim we should have in sharing the gospel message with others?
>
> ❷ How hard is this work?
>
> ❷ Where does the strength come from?

We slog... and he sustains. But it helps when we are clear about the basics. Jesus is our message. Our aim is to bring people to maturity in Christ for eternity.

Pray

Pray that this would be your aim and the aim of those in your church who lead. Pray they would work hard and rely on God.

Bible in a year: Isaiah 51 • Jeremiah 30 • Jonah 2 • 1 Timothy 4

Protective measures

In Colossians 2 Paul will go on to talk about the threats to a Christian's maturity in Christ. But as with any disease, the best cure is prevention...

Read Colossians 2:1-5

❷ *What does Paul want for the Christians he knows and does not know?*

❷ *Why is his prayer for these things so urgent (v 4)?*

Objectives like encouragement and unity trip off the tongue so easily that they can quickly become clichés. So Paul has to contend in prayer for them. That is not simply because it is hard to keep praying and working for people you have never met, but also because neither encouragement nor unity come easily. They have to be fought for. C.S. Lewis once said, "Everyone thinks forgiveness is a lovely idea until he has something to forgive". Something similar could be said for unity—it's a lovely idea until we find something to divide over. That is when loving a brother or sister in Christ becomes a challenge. Furthermore, the implication

is that unity is related to how "encouraged in heart" we might be. This is not the limp idea of generally feeling upbeat; the phrase has the sense of being strengthened and fortified—literally, being instilled with courage.

⬇ Apply

❷ *How do encouragement, unity and understanding prevent us from being deceived?*

❷ *How would you put Paul's prayer priorities in the diagram below into your own words?*

⬆ Pray

Use Paul's pattern below to pray for two people you know, and two Christians you have never met before.

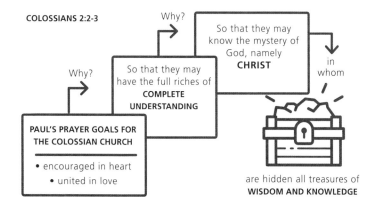

COLOSSIANS 2:2-3

Why? → So that they may know the mystery of God, namely **CHRIST** → in whom

Why? → So that they may have the full riches of **COMPLETE UNDERSTANDING**

PAUL'S PRAYER GOALS FOR THE COLOSSIAN CHURCH

• encouraged in heart
• united in love

are hidden all treasures of **WISDOM AND KNOWLEDGE**

Look at, look through

It is a stark truth that makes us feel uncomfortable—death mocks everything. But beginning to wrestle with that stark truth is the only way to look at life as it really is.

Keeping quiet

Read Psalm 39:1-3

❷ *What did David do "while in the presence of the wicked"?*

❷ *How did this make him feel?*

In the psalms, "wicked" is often simply a term for "non-believer". David knows that sharing his "anguish" with those who don't love God will be unhelpful. They may mock him, or give him false assurance.

But the longer he stays quiet, the worse he feels. So he turns to speak.

Speaking out

Read Psalm 39:4-11

❷ *To whom does David speak (v 4)?*

❷ *What do these verses reveal as the cause of David's anguish (v 4-6, 11)?*

The problem with life is death. Our days are numbered, and brief (v 5); and our possessions are only on loan to us (v 6). To realise "how fleeting my life is" is a spiritual gift, something to be prayed for (v 4).

❷ *What does understanding the reality of death cause David to do (v 7)?*

❷ *If he ignored the reality of death, do you think he would have put his hope in that place? Why/why not?*

Many things promise to be a good vessel for our hope—our confidence for the present

and the future. But ultimately, none of them can change the truth that life is "a mere handbreadth" (v 5). Where do we look once we acknowledge that death mocks all our achievements and accumulations? To God: "my hope is in you" (v 7). Nothing else carries any hope the day after our death. And we'll only appreciate this if we accept the reality, and feel the wrongness, of death.

Too much?

Read Psalm 39:12-13

❷ *What does David feel like (v 12)?*

Foreigners were allowed to live in Israel, but not to own land there. Here, the King of Israel declares himself a foreigner! David's point is that, in this God-created world, he is just passing through. This is not where we belong, and not where we can stay.

Verse 13 is strange! But perhaps David simply cannot bear to think about the stark truth of death any longer. But as we look at death, we have a great gift that David did not own—knowledge of the resurrection. We don't look at death—we look through it. **Read John 11:25-26.**

Pray

Pray Psalm 39:4 for yourself. Thank God that this is not the final word, because you look forward to being alive in glory beyond death, and not merely to being "no more".

The secret of growth

What is the secret of growing into maturity as a Christian? Paul will go on to talk about three false ways, but first he presents the real way…

As you received…

Read Colossians 2:6

❓ *How does Paul describe how to become a Christian here?*

"You received Christ Jesus as Lord." The words might trip off the tongue, but they contain a wealth of detail. "Christ Jesus" tells us that we are committed to someone who actually lived in history—not an idea, a story or a myth but a living, breathing person. And the belief that he is "Lord" is our conviction that he is God's chosen King and Lord of all. But more than that, becoming a Christian is *personal*. We "receive" him. It is not just ticking off a list of facts we believe about Christ. It is receiving him personally into our lives that makes us true Christians.

… continue

Read Colossians 2:6 again

❓ *What is the secret of going on in the Christian life?*

Paul's word in verse 6 often translated "live" literally means "walk". We are to continue walking with him and in him. The secret of *growing* as a Christian is precisely the same as *becoming* a Christian: daily receiving Christ Jesus as Lord and living out the implications of that. John Stott used to say that we should each "daily bewail our sin and daily adore our Saviour".

Rooted and built up

Read Colossians 2:6-7

❓ *What two pictures of growing as a Christian does Paul use in verse 7?*

❓ *What does he say the experience of living as a believer should be?*

Grounded. Convinced. Unshakable. Thankful. These are the marks of a mature Christian believer. With strong roots, like a mature tree, we will not be blown over by a hurricane. Like a well-built house, we will have strong foundations and remain standing even when an earthquake rocks us.

Paul uses one further metaphor from the natural world—a river that has burst its banks. The torrents of rainwater are unstoppable and they flow wherever they can. Likewise, the gratitude of those who have received Christ Jesus as Lord knows no bounds. But perhaps that seems unrealistic—especially when life is hard or confusing. How could gratitude overflow then? The answer is because of what motivates that gratitude: the privilege and wonder of knowing Christ and his grace.

⌄ Apply

❓ *On these criteria and by these measures are you growing as a Christian?*

Spend some time expressing your overflowing gratitude to God.

Fake news

Paul now turns to some of the storms that seek to undermine our confident faith in Christ. He introduces them with a summary statement of what is at stake.

Hollow and deceptive

Read Colossians 2:8

❓ *How does Paul describe the things that threaten to knock us off course as Christians?*

❓ *What is the fundamental flaw with them?*

❓ *Why might these things be so deceptive—even for Christians?*

Fly fishing rests on pure deception. A replica of an insect is flicked over the surface of the river, luring an unsuspecting fish into rising to the surface for the next tasty insect morsel. The more convincing the fly, the better it will work. So it is with the fake news of false teaching. If it didn't resemble the real thing, people would never be taken in. What resembles good food is actually a trap. It promises the earth but delivers nothing. It is all surface with little substance.

It may come with the weight of substantial human traditions behind it: magnificent buildings and an impressive history. It may come with a sense of real "spiritual power" about it. But at the end of the day it does not rest on Christ.

The real deal

Read Colossians 2:9-15

❓ *What arguments does Paul use to show how superior Jesus is to the fake alternatives?*

❓ *What has happened to us as believers joined to Christ (v 12)?*

❓ *What three enemies are destroyed by Jesus' death on the cross (v 13-15)? How has this been achieved?*

Paul piles on the arguments, starting with a recap of his statements about who Jesus is from Colossians 1. The mention of circumcision here perhaps reflects that the Christians were being pulled away by false Jewish teaching. He explains that the only circumcision that matters is the one that we receive in Christ—we are spiritually joined in Christ to the people of God. We are made alive in Christ as we join him in his death and his resurrection. We were forgiven *all* our sins (2:13). And the impressive spiritual powers that lie behind alternative philosophies were defeated utterly by Christ on the cross. The implication is clear. Tempting though they are, why would you want to swap Jesus for them?

⌄ Apply

❓ *What human philosophies and traditions do you think you and your church are particularly vulnerable to believing? How do they tempt us into thinking that Jesus is not enough?*

❓ *What kinds of things are we tempted to "add" to faith in Christ in order to give us more assurance? What is the antidote to these claims?*

Bible in a year: Acts 19 • 1 Corinthians 7 – 8

Legalists and mystics

False teaching attacks our heads, hearts or hands. Wrong thinking. Wrong feelings. Or a wrong attitude towards the significance of what we do with our bodies.

Don't judge me!

Read Colossians 2:16-17

- ❓ *What do the things listed in verse 16 have in common?*
- ❓ *What do you imagine the situation is in Colossae, from verse 16?*
- ❓ *Why would the Christians find that difficult?*
- ❓ *What should they say to themselves and their accusers (v 17)?*

These practices were all issues touched on in the old covenant. In their different ways, each of these were the means for Old Testament believers to show their devotion to, and dependence on, their rescuer God. It proved they were different from their pagan neighbours, for whom such laws were irrelevant. So in a sense, the whole point was that people did judge believers by these things! If you didn't follow these rules, people would assume you were not part of the devout in-crowd. But now Paul suggests that none of it matters anymore. They were just the shadows, and the reality is Christ. When you have the real thing, you don't need the shadow.

✔ Apply

- ❓ *Perhaps we are not troubled by Jewish laws and rituals, but what are some of the rules we lay on each other?*
- ❓ *What should we say to ourselves and our accusers when we are judged?*

Don't disqualify me!

Read Colossians 2:18-19

- ❓ *What are the twin practises that Paul talks about here?*
- ❓ *Why might believers feel threatened by these things?*
- ❓ *What is Paul's conclusion about those who encourage these things?*

Verse 18 refers not to worshipping angels—no true Christian would be tempted by that—but the claim to worship *alongside* angels. In other words, these people were experiencing a profound intimacy with God through their times of worship, and so they argued that those who didn't join in with them were truly missing out. The suggestion is that they went through elaborate, self-denying processes (extended periods of fasting or extra-long prayer times perhaps) in order to enter into the "right space" for worship and participate in a higher kind of worship. This is a kind of mystical experience available only to those dedicated to going through all the right techniques. But in doing so, Paul says, they have lost connection with Christ. We are already in him and he is in us. No rituals, no special experiences, no self-denial is needed. We live and move in his presence all the time.

✦ Pray

Enjoy the full and free access to God the Father that you have in Christ now.

Dead but alive

Legalism is alive and well—if not in our churches, then in a corner of our minds. It is the voice that tells us, "If you don't do this or that, you're not a real believer…"

Dead to law

Read Colossians 2:20-23

❷ *What does Paul say has happened to all Christians?*

❷ *What are the implications of this for how we think about rules?*

❷ *What particular rules does Paul seem to have in mind (v 21-22)?*

❷ *What two big reasons or principles does Paul give in verse 22 to reject these rules?*

❷ *What is so attractive about these rules (v 23)?*

Of course, it's rarely that simple. Many of the rules, practices and customs that build up around our expectations of what Christian spirituality and discipleship look like have their origins in Scripture. And skilled exponents will make a wise case for why we must fall in line. But even if such rules have their origins in Scripture, legalism twists them into something thoroughly worldly. They are "based on merely human commands and teachings". They will perish because they are past their sell-by date. They are from a past era: the shadow times. But now the mystery has been revealed and we live with the reality—Christ.

⌄ Apply

So here's the shock: *it is worldly to be religious!* This is why religious legalism should be entirely out of place for the Christian believer. We are to enjoy our security and freedom and not regress back to the old way of thinking.

But this is hard, precisely because the legalistic mindset runs so deeply within us. Countering it sometimes needs conscious efforts—the deliberate decision to resist the accusing voices of our minds that try to convince us of divine disappointment and thus our spiritual jeopardy. We must stop ourselves. We must say to ourselves, *No! That's just worldliness! God's love for me does not depend on my spiritual and moral performance! It depends on Christ dying for me.*

This is a lifelong battle—so we should not be caught by surprise. Legalism is normal and ingrained thinking. But it is emphatically not Christian thinking.

The irony of legalism

Read Colossians 2:23

❷ *Why does legalism ultimately fail?*

If we imagine that we can control our most sinful impulses and desires by being obsessively religious, and can do so without Christ, then Paul has strong words for us. *It won't work.* Observers might greatly respect us (as the people of Jesus' time did the Pharisees). Or they might despise us and assume that we are perfectly insane. Either way, this approach is proved to be utterly pointless.

Bible in a year: 2 Corinthians 2, 4, 7

A new address

"Where are you from?" It is the first question we ask on meeting someone who seems "different". Christians have a radical answer to that question.

Where are you?

Read Colossians 3:1-4

❓ *Where do Christians live now?*

❓ *How did we get there?*

❓ *When will our identity be fully and finally revealed?*

❓ *How does Paul say this truth should shape our thinking?*

When Jesus rose from the dead, those in Christ rose with him. Where he goes, we go. The extraordinary thing is that because Jesus then ascended to his heavenly throne and sat down, we have too. In Christ, we are in heaven. Already. That is our true home. It is only natural, therefore, to seek after what Paul literally calls "the above things" (v 2). This must include the things that make the heavenly realms so wonderful, joyful and magnetic: the wonder of spending time with Christ, the one we love and adore—everything that flows from being in the place "where Christ is". So Paul instructs the Colossians to set their hearts on these things. This means to meditate on them, value them, prioritise them. Above all, let them shape and influence life in the here and now.

⌄ Apply

❓ *Write down all the "identities" you possess (nationality, job, relationships, etc.). Honestly, put them in the order they seem most important to you. Where does your identity in Christ sit in the list? Why is that, and how can it be made the highest priority?*

A new wardrobe

Read Colossians 3:5-11

❓ *Why is it important to understand the lessons on legalism in Colossians 2 as we read these verses?*

❓ *What three pictures does Paul use to show us how to live as new people in Christ (v 5, 7, 8-9)?*

❓ *What do the things listed in verses 5 and 8-9 have in common?*

Growing as a Christian is not so much about desperately trying to stop doing things. It is primarily about seeing what Christ has done for and in us, and realising that we are dead to the old things. We now walk in a different direction. We have taken off our old clothes and put on some glorious new ones to wear to the Lamb's wedding feast. Paul is saying, *Be who you are.* Nowhere is this new way of living clearer than in our attitudes towards sex and in how we speak: in our relationships with others.

⌃ Pray

Thank God for who he has made you in Christ; and talk to him about the lists in verses 5 and 8-9.

Bible in a year: 2 Corinthains 8 – 9 • Titus 3

A new family

We do not seek to grow in holiness out of fear. Fear is what religion provokes, because it stirs up anxiety about what God might do to us when we fail.

Christians long to grow in holiness *out of confidence*—we belong to God because we are united to Christ. It is simply a matter of being who we have been saved to be.

Relationships

Read Colossians 3:8-11

❷ *What does verse 11 add to the perspective that Paul is building up of our new life in Christ?*

❷ *How do you think Paul's original hearers might have responded to verse 11?*

The proof of the Christian's conversion is in their interactions with others. It is almost impossible to grow as a disciple in isolation. But the church fellowship is not simply formed of other people who are like us. The church was never designed to be a club for like-minded or same-cultured people. Jesus is frustratingly unfussy about who he chooses and loves. He does not discriminate, which is why it is worse than a tragedy when Christians do. It suggests we think we are somehow superior to some of those for whom Christ died—as if we were more deserving somehow, when the truth is that none of us deserve for it to be this good.

We easily lose sight of how revolutionary verse 11 really is. Our connection to Christ puts all other identities in their place—no matter how proud or patriotic we may be, our first kingdom is always the kingdom of Christ: King Jesus is all.

Realities

Read Colossians 3:12-14

❷ *How does it help our relationships with others to know that we are chosen ... holy ... dearly loved (v 12)?*

❷ *What practical reality regarding relationships is Paul pointing to in these verses?*

There are always going to be members of the church community who require from us very big hearts if we are to put up with them. People can be irritating, frustrating, hurtful and cutting—*and so can you!* And you will be painfully aware that forgiveness is easier to think about than it is to actually do. That's why Paul points us to our own need for forgiveness and the example of our Lord Jesus, who sacrificed all for our forgiveness (v 13). We so desperately need the love of God poured into our hearts for each other.

⌄ Apply

❷ *Endure, forgive, love... Which of these do people find hardest to do in your fellowship? Why is it so corrosive to a church's life and witness when these things are not practised?*

⌃ Pray

Ask God to help you love others, and that your church would model the things we have read about today.

Lifted from the pit

Real life is a mixture of praising God for his salvation and help, and praying to him for salvation and help. It was no different for David.

A new song

Read Psalm 40:1-10

> ❷ *Why is David praising God (v 1)? How does the image of v 2 bring this to life?*

The footnote for verse 4 is striking. Blessing lies in trusting the true God, who alone can truly hear us and rescue us. The alternative is to "turn aside to false gods/lies". Beware the sweet-talking, smooth-lying false god who promises to lift you up but in fact leaves you in the pit.

> ❷ *What does David suggest God most desires (v 6, 8)?*

Hebrew writing often makes a point through over-comparison (see Jesus' words in Luke 14:26). So it is not that God does not want sacrifices and offerings (or he would not have inspired Leviticus!)—but God does care far more about our hearts' devotion than our hands' offerings.

> ❷ *What does David do in response to what God has done for him (Psalm 40:9-10)?*

When was the last time you shared the goodness of God to you in your "assembly"—your church? How strange it is when we experience God's help, and "hide" it from others who would be encouraged by it!

An urgent prayer

Read Psalm 40:11-17

> ❷ *How does the tone change here?*

> ❷ *What two problems does David have (v 12)?*

So David prays for help—and it is because he has already experienced verses 1-2 that he is able to pray confidently in verse 17. He has been saved and helped; now he needs to be saved and helped. His only question in verse 17 is about when God will help, but not about whether he will.

The perfect version

In verses 6-8, David almost seems to be speaking about a perfect version of himself. And he is! **Read Luke 4:16-21; Hebrews 10:5-10.** The one written about in the "scroll" of God's law and prophecy is not David. The one who perfectly desired to do God's will is not David. The one who offered himself so that God truly did not desire or require any further sacrifice is not David. *It is Jesus.* And so it is Jesus who enables us to sing the ultimate and eternal new song—of being lifted from the slime of our sin and the pit of our shame, and given a firm place to stand on the ground around his throne.

⌃ Pray

> ❷ *What difficulty or disappointment are you facing in life today?*

Reflect on what Jesus has done for you, using the words of Psalm 40:1-2. Praise him in song (perhaps your favourite hymn). Then pray verse 17 with confidence.

How to do church

In a Christian community, we are not shaped by rules, but we are shaped by our Ruler.
His rule is unlike any other. It is a rule of genuine peace.

True peace

Read Colossians 3:15-17

❓ *What do you think it means to "let the peace of Christ rule in [our] hearts"?*

❓ *How does that happen among us, according to verse 16?*

❓ *What is the repeated command in these verses? Why do you think that is?*

Conflict will always arise when two or more people are together. But conflict among believers is not by itself the problem, but the way it gets handled can be. The key in Paul's mind here seems to be Christ's peace ruling "in your hearts". This is not super-spiritual escapism, as if we simply need to meditate on Jesus and feel peaceful before an argument. Since the heart is the source of all those passions and lusts which cause so many problems in the world, and which Paul referred to in verses 5-9, he is saying that Christ must rule there. The peace he achieved on the cross to reconcile us to God and to each other must be the decisive factor in any dispute.

The mindset of gratitude has been one of the letter's consistent themes (look back to 1:12 and 2:7). It is wholly appropriate here. If every individual involved in a church dispute insisted on returning to what he or she was thankful to God for, it would guarantee that their relationships would be profoundly improved. It would put our identity in Christ centre stage—and thereby make it

more likely that people would bear with and forgive one another (3:13). And essential to the whole process is that we are sitting under the gospel message together—"the message of Christ".

True worship

Read Colossians 3:15-17 again

❓ *What is practically involved in letting the message of Christ dwell in us richly?*

❓ *What role does Paul say singing should play in our lives together?*

There should be a horizontal as well as a vertical dimension to our singing. We sing to God of course, with gratitude in our hearts. But there should also be a way that the words of the songs shape our thinking, and even rebuke us for our sinful behaviour. Notice also that *variety* in singing was important right from the beginning.

✔ Apply

❓ *What are the three ingredients for a healthy Christian life (v 15, 16, 17)? How do you think you match up to these criteria? What about your church?*

⌃ Pray

Ask God to help you enjoy his peace and be an agent of his peace as you meet with your brothers and sisters this week.

How to do family

*To our ears, these brief but punchy commands may seem dated and even dangerous. This is why we need to see what Paul is and, more significantly, is **not** saying.*

Home truths

Household codes were not unusual in the ancient world. But they shared one thing in common: women, slaves and children were all "owned"—the father was the undisputed authority in the home.

Read Colossians 3:18 – 4:1

❓ *What is the common thread that runs through these commands (3:18, 20, 22-23)?*

❓ *What are the big surprises in verses 19, 21 and 22?*

In cities around the Roman world, women (v 18) and slaves (v 22-24), and their children (v 20), were being converted. God was at work among them. Not only that: God was using women and slaves, and no doubt also children, to further his kingdom. So just as Jesus did before him, Paul shows them the respect due to those with minds and wills of their own. This was revolutionary. No one had ever done that before. Every previous household code had been addressed deliberately and exclusively to the male head of the house. Furthermore, Paul addresses each of these less powerful groups first.

A word to Dad

Read Colossians 3:18 – 4:1 again

❓ *What role does the father have in the household?*

❓ *Who is the true head of the household?*

A pagan teacher would give all kinds of helpful tips for how such a man could get the best out of the household team. That might include treating his subordinates well enough so that they would do what he wanted. But the emphasis was consistent: it helped *him* keep order among *them*. There's not a bit of this with Paul. *Not once*—either here or in his other household codes—does Paul ever tell the men to *make* the women, children or slaves do *anything*. This is a fact overlooked by too many men who rule their homes like petty dictators, even justifying physical violence on the basis of these verses. They want to force everyone else to bend to their will. Instead, Paul gives some profoundly challenging and even subversive instructions to the men. They are not the head of the household: Jesus is. And we all play out our roles in submission to Christ.

✅ Apply

❓ *Identify one personal relationship you are struggling with at the moment. What command from these verses do you most need to hear and work through right now?*

❓ *How does the centrality of Jesus to all our relationships change everything?*

Prayer and partnership

We have access to God in prayer by the grace we have received in Christ. Why then do we so often find it difficult to pray?

Devoted

Read Colossians 4:2

❓ *What do you think it means in practice to "devote yourselves to prayer"?*

❓ *What do you think being watchful involves?*

Yet again, Paul is not laying down the law here. He is not offering a list of rules and regulations by which we can measure our efforts; for prayerfulness can only be motivated by a response to God's grace. That's why we want to spend time with God! That's why Paul uses a word like "devote" (v 2). It suggests our sincere passion as much as our deliberate purpose. Sometimes there is a battle between our passion and our purpose, when we are distracted by other things that might be good in themselves to do but that drag us away from our prayer times. What matters is that we each find a way to spend time in prayer, using whatever methods that genuinely help. There are no rules, but we can develop good disciplines.

⌄ Apply

Prayer doesn't need to be in a closed room. You can pray when out for a walk, or by using a list or a smartphone app to keep a record of your prayer commitments.

❓ *Where's the best place for you to pray? If you struggle to make the time, work out why that is and come up with a solution.*

Praying for the gospel

Read Colossians 4:3-6

❓ *What is Paul's prayer request in his mission to proclaim the gospel?*

❓ *What other advice does Paul give us for how we relate to "not-yet Christians"?*

❓ *What is the implication of Paul's use of the word "conversation" in verse 6?*

Paul wants opportunities (open doors) to share the good news about Jesus. But he also wants clarity when he is speaking. How much we need the same things ourselves! But he also knows that it is God who gives these things, and that it is God's work to make new disciples of Christ. Paul expects people to talk with family, friends and neighbours. He longs for us to feel as comfortable with talking about Jesus as we might about our jobs or the sports results. Conversation implies dialogue and mutual interest, which hopefully means saying things that prompt questions. "Seasoned with salt" seems to have been an old Jewish idiom for keeping things interesting. That can be through being quirky, or provocative, or surprising. The key is to avoid being predictable or banal, because we long for conversation to lead to a new recognition that Christ is indeed Lord.

⌃ Pray

Pray for open doors, clarity and fruitful conversations.

The gospel team

The themes of this letter have been cosmic: Jesus Christ, the image of God, who is Lord of all. But the application is always personal and relational...

Unity and diversity

Read Colossians 4:7-18

❓ *Despite Paul and Aristarchus being in prison, what is the tone and feel of this last section of the letter? What do you put that down to?*

❓ *What is striking about the people Paul mentions? Think about their names and backgrounds.*

❓ *What is sad about verse 14 (see 2 Timothy 4:10)?*

There is not a hint of self-pity here. Paul does not ask that they pray for him to be let out. He is simply bubbling over with enthusiasm and delight in the group of Christians God has pulled around him, which means the gospel mission goes on. Tychichus may have had a lot of other things to tell them (Colossians 4:7), but none of these details is as important as the contents of the letter.

The gospel team in Ephesus (the likely place Paul was in prison), and the churches of Colossae and Laodicea contain a wonderful mix of people that put the truth of 3:11 on display. Three Jewish men (4:10-11); three Gentiles (Epaphras, Luke and Demas)—probably Greek; Onesimus the runaway slave, and then the women at Colossae, including Nympha (v 15). All are spoken *to* and *of* on a level playing field. We are all one in Christ Jesus.

The sad fact is that Demas, at some stage,

fell away. Even those at the very heart of a thriving gospel ministry are vulnerable to temptation.

⬇ Apply

❓ *How diverse is your church? What might be the reasons for this?*

❓ *How does Epaphras' prayer in verse 12 sum up what the letter is about?*

A summary prayer

Read Colossians 4:12

Epaphras' prayer is one that we might use for everyone we know: that Christians would stand firm, grow into maturity, and have complete assurance of the truth of the gospel and their unity with Christ. God's grace can only provoke our gratitude to God. And our gratitude must surely work out in graciousness to one and all, whether to those who are part of the body, or towards outsiders who ply us with questions.

Grace. Gratitude. Graciousness. This is lordship the like of which the world has never seen. What an extraordinary privilege to know it first hand. So as Christ has shared his grace with us, we, with Paul, share grace with all.

⬆ Pray

Use Epaphras' prayer as a model to pray for those you know.

CHRISTMAS: True story

Strange visitations by angelic beings and then a mysterious birth to a virgin? God becoming man?! Stories like this were common in the ancient world, but this is different…

Roving researcher

Read Luke 1:1-4

❓ *What does Luke want his first readers to get from his Gospel (v 4)?*

❓ *What does he say in these verses that would give them (and us) this confidence?*

❓ *What methods did Luke use to compile his account?*

Luke claims to have written a work of investigative journalism. He has carefully searched through by using the following:

- **Written reports.** It seems they were not short of documents in the ancient world that recorded the teaching and other details of Jesus' life and death. He says that there were "many" (v 1). But Luke doesn't just take these as "gospel"…

- **Eyewitnesses.** He talks to those who were actually there. His gospel narrative isn't cobbled together from things that happened to "a friend of a friend". *No.* Luke takes the trouble to check out, and presumably correct and supplement the earlier written documents by interviewing people who were actually there.

- **Careful investigation.** Luke, who is elsewhere described as a physician (Colossians 4:14), is clearly a man of serious learning, with an enquiring mind. He pieces together the various bits of evidence and writes them up as an "orderly account". This means that it is grouped in an organised way, not necessarily written in the order that it happened.

···· TIME OUT ·······································

Theophilus (a Greek name meaning "lover of God") may have been a wealthy patron who Luke sent his Gospel to. Or it could be that this is a kind of code word for God's people, i.e. that it was written for the early church—those who love God.

Truth teller

Re-read Luke 1:1

But Luke says he's doing more than just recording events—he's writing about the things that have been "fulfilled" (NIV) or "accomplished" (ESV) among them. He reminds us that these events of Jesus' birth, life, death and resurrection are part of something much bigger. They are part of the story of God's dealing with mankind from the very beginning, and how the fact of Jesus coming into the world changes everything, for everyone, for all time.

Pray

We all sometimes feel that the Bible is a bit "unreal". Pray that, as you read Luke's account of Jesus' birth, you will become more convinced of its historical truth. And pray that this Christmastime, you would have opportunities to tell others about the reality of Jesus and what he accomplished for us.

Silent witness

Like no other Gospel writer, Luke tells us the remarkable events leading up to Jesus' birth, weaving into his account the birth of Jesus' forerunner, John the Baptist.

After his introduction, where he is at pains to underline that he is writing history, Luke introduces us to John's parents.

Godly but childless

Read Luke 1:5-10

- ❓ *What kind of people were Zechariah and Elizabeth?*
- ❓ *How would their childlessness have been viewed by their culture (see v 25)?*
- ❓ *How might they have viewed it themselves, do you think?*

To be childless was a sure sign, so people imagined, of God's rejection. But does that fit with verse 6? It's not the message of verse 9 either; it was a great once-in-a-lifetime privilege to burn incense, and guess who controlled the lot which chose Zechariah for this task!

Your prayer is heard

Read Luke 1:11-13

While the crowds were waiting outside, Zechariah was having the shock of his life. And the angel's message was as startling as his appearance. A baby! But they'd long given up hope... It was impossible... They were old people—and yet God had heard those heartfelt prayers after all. And what an answer he was about to give them!

- ❓ *What does that teach us about all those prayers you thought God hadn't noticed?*

It's a great mistake to assume that God is angry or absent when we go through deep trouble. God brought Elizabeth's richest blessing through her most painful trial.

Powerful promise

Read Luke 1:14-25

- ❓ *What remarkable promises does the angel give about the child?*
- ❓ *How should Zechariah have responded to this promise?*
- ❓ *What do we learn about God's promises by the way the story plays out?*

The child would bring tremendous joy (v 14)—not just to the astonished and delighted parents, but to many others too. He would also be great in God's eyes (v 15), and filled with God's Spirit. Devout and devoted parents all want their children to exceed their own devotion to God. Elizabeth and Zechariah's prayers would be powerfully answered, as their son would be God's instrument for bringing revival to Israel.

🔼 Pray

God is not reluctant to answer prayer. It's just that he has far greater plans in mind than we do. Prayer is not trying to coax a reluctant God to give us what we want, but yielding ourselves to the will of God, who has far bigger ambitions for us than we can imagine.

Bible in a year: John 6, 10, 12

The God of the weak

God is compassionate. And compassion cares for the weak, works for the betrayed, and blesses the broken. This psalm celebrates that God does all those things.

It also points us to a surprising place to prove that he does.

Have regard

Read Psalm 41:1-3

> ❓ *What does God do for "the weak" (v 1-3)?*

The verbs here are wonderfully comforting if you are feeling "weak" today. The Lord delivers, protects, preserves, sustains, restores. These verses are, of course, not promising that God will never allow a weak or sick person to die (David himself would die in bed, 1 Kings 2:10). But they are an assurance that when we are at our weakest, we will find God there and experience his compassion in those times, if we have eyes to see it and a heart to welcome it.

Sinned-against sinner

Read Psalm 41:4-9

> ❓ *What kind of people are surrounding David (v 5-9)?*
>
> ❓ *What else is he keenly aware of (v 4)?*

David (as in the last psalm) holds his own sin and others' unjust treatment of him together, but it is not that one is necessarily caused by the other; it is that both are the usual experience of the follower of God. Being treated unjustly is not a punishment for our sin; equally, being treated unjustly is not an excuse for our sin.

Raise me up

Read Psalm 41:10-13

> ❓ *What does David...*
> • *ask for (v 10)?*
> • *feel assured of (v 11-12)?*

In verse 12, David seems to be contrasting his own "integrity" of heart with others' slanderous hearts (v 6). God upholds the person who relies on God, not on plotting.

The ultimate weak one

Surely Jesus had verse 9 in mind as he discussed his betrayal with his disciples—**read Mark 14:17-21.** In fact, the only verse in the whole of Psalm 41 that Jesus could not have said was verse 4—he would suffer for others' sins, not his own. He was the weak one, the betrayed one, the broken one. And he is the risen one—the one whom his Father compassionately raised from the dead, to triumph over his enemies and to enjoy his Father's pleasure for ever. The empty tomb proves that God "has regard" for those who are weak, yet walk with integrity of heart.

⌃ Pray

Thank the Father that he had regard for his Son, raising him from the dead. Thank the Son that he had regard for you, dying to raise you from your spiritual death-bed. Pray that you, in your turn, would "have regard for the weak".

Big baby

Gabriel's second task was to bear news far more staggering and wonderful than the first message. And to whom would the angel be sent? An ordinary young woman.

Highly favoured

Read Luke 1:26-30

❷ *The appearance of an angel is troubling, but what is Mary disturbed by (v 29)?*

What a proof that God loves the humble! Mary had nothing going for her, humanly speaking. She lived in the despised town of Nazareth and was engaged to a lowly carpenter. We can readily understand Mary being startled by the angel suddenly appearing. But it's Gabriel's words that bother her most; "troubled" that she, of all women, could be counted favoured by God! What beautiful humility shines from Mary's whole response.

❷ *Had she forgotten the truth of Isaiah 57:15?*

Mind-blowing

Read Luke 1:31-34

❷ *Weigh the words of Gabriel's promises to Mary. What does each phrase mean?*

❷ *What does her response tell us about her attitude and character?*

If Mary was amazed that she had been favoured by God, imagine how her mind would be reeling when the angel explained just what that would mean... Mary surely did not grasp the full significance of what was being said. She did not have time to stop and think through each phrase to appreciate its wonder. But we can take it more slowly; this glorious King of kings growing from a human embryo to a full-grown baby in the womb of an ordinary girl.

Mary believed that it would happen as the angel had said, but how? Was she to marry Joseph first? The angel's reply would certainly be a severe test of her faith...

Heavenly conception

Read Luke 1:35-38

❷ *Weigh the words of Gabriel's promises to Mary. What does each phrase mean?*

❷ *What does her response tell us about her attitude and character?*

Consider the wonder of conception. The intricate complexity of a fully functioning human springing from two tiny cells—male and female. But the origin of Mary's child would be totally different, conceived by God's Holy Spirit. He would have no other biological father than God—an awesome thought for Mary to come to terms with.

Mary must face the stigma of being pregnant, but not married. Probably her family would reject her, and surely Joseph would now despise her. But Mary does not seem to be worried; there is a beautiful serenity about her reply. No objections about the difficulties, no further questions about how all these things could happen. Just a desire to be the Lord's servant, just a quiet submission to her Lord's will.

Good news shared

Mary was quick to follow up the news brought by the angel; she couldn't wait to share the good news with Elizabeth.

Spirit-filled

Read Luke 1:39-45

Whether or not Mary spilled the beans in her greeting, it was not she who convinced Elizabeth of the truth…

❓ *Who did?*

❓ *What else did the Spirit reveal to her?*

❓ *How did this Spirit-filled woman encourage her cousin?*

When believers are filled with God's Holy Spirit, they begin to overflow. Elizabeth could not help crying out with joy and worship. But notice what form this takes: she is filled with the sense of her own unworthiness, and with wonder that God should bring such blessing to her.

Blessing and honour

Read Luke 1:46-56

❓ *What were the blessings Mary was overwhelmed with?*

❓ *What earth-shattering impact does she see her child would have on the world?*

❓ *What words does she use to describe the character of God in this song?*

❓ *Why did these truths particularly thrill Mary, do you think?*

❓ *How has God acted in respect of his promises?*

❓ *In verses 50-54, how has he acted towards "those who fear him" (those who are needy)? And towards the proud?*

Verse 47 could indicate that Mary was already looking to her baby as the one who would save her from her sins, though her understanding would have been rather hazy.

She knew that God is mighty, holy, merciful. These were not just words in Mary's mind, as they can be in our prayers. Expressions of God's character are embedded in the prayers you find in the Bible. They are the source of so much praise, and the grounds for our motivation to pray. If you want to praise God, then spend time considering who he is.

It's hard to separate who he is from what he does—for God's character is always expressed in how he acts.

🔼 Pray

❓ *Has God done "great things" for you? What exactly?*

❓ *Has he brought about wonderful changes in your life? Has he shown Jesus to be your Saviour?*

If so, then verse 47 is yours as well. Mary spills out reasons to praise God because her heart is bursting with love for God's amazing grace.

It's a great moment for you to do the same…

Bible in a year: 1 Timothy 5 • 2 Timothy 1 – 2

Birthday surprise

As today, the birth of a child was a time of tremendous joy and interest, not just for the family but for friends and neighbours too.

And it is easy to imagine the stir caused by a couple the age of Elizabeth and Zechariah having a child. Evidently the family wanted a say in choosing the name too...

His name is John

Read Luke 1:57-63

Zechariah was such an appropriate name (meaning "The Lord has remembered"); it was usual to take a family name and the family would be offended otherwise. But there was no room for manoeuvre; Elizabeth and Zechariah were clear—"His name is John". They were not being obstinate; God had made it clear to them in verse 13.

But why John? Surely the forerunner of Jesus was called John for a special reason. John means "The Lord is gracious".

> ❷ *Why is this name especially appropriate? Think about who John was to be.*

What kind of child?

Read Luke 1:64-66

> ❷ *How did the people react?*

> ❷ *What things were making them think?*

The people had been astonished at the parents' choice—and their boldness. But now they could clearly see that God was at work and had a great purpose for the child.

⌄ Apply

If God's word is clear, then we mustn't listen to the persuasive arguments of others who follow what the culture deems to be acceptable!

"They'll be offended"
"We've always done it this way"
"It will cause embarrassment"

Be one of the few who stands up, clearly but graciously, for what God's word says.

> ❷ *What might this need to look like for you specifically in the run-up to Christmas this year?*

⌃ Pray

We do well to notice events showing that hint that God is at work; to react with awe, to wonder, to tell others what God is doing.

Plead with God that once again he will do things in our lives, in our churches and in our land which will make people really sit up and take notice—so they have to admit: "Surely God is with you; and there is no other".

Prophetic poem

Zechariah made good use of the voice God had given back to him. You can imagine how thankful he was for the gift of his son, John; but John only gets two verses!

Zechariah's best praise is for another child...

Praise him for salvation

Read Luke 1:67-75

> ❓ *What were God's great purposes in sending to earth Jesus, the "horn of salvation"? List the things that Jesus would accomplish.*

The language might reflect Zechariah's rather "Israel-based" understanding of the Messiah. But the Holy Spirit inspired him to say rather more than he realised...

🔼 Pray

God's work in salvation through Jesus is the theme of Zechariah's praise—is it ours? Use the headings below to shape your praises as you reflect on the indescribable gift of God's Son.

- He redeems his people (v 68, 69).
- He saves us from our enemies (v 71).
- He keeps his promises (v 72, 73).
- He frees his people to serve him (v 74-75).

Can you thank God for Jesus from the bottom of your heart, knowing that you are one of his people for whom he has such great purposes? If not, then don't be satisfied until you can.

Two verses for his son

Read Luke 1:76-77

> ❓ *What will be the life's work of Zechariah's son?*

Even at this joyful moment for Dad, Zechariah is doing what his son would do—pointing to Jesus! Even the verses about John speak of him preparing the way for Jesus.

John was the prophet who would prepare the way for the Saviour, stirring up the people to be ready for him.

Then back to Jesus

Read Luke 1:78-79

Zechariah is overwhelmed again by God's amazing mercy in sending Jesus.

> ❓ *How is the picture of the rising sun such a beautiful and appropriate picture of the coming of Jesus into the lives of sinners?*

🔽 Apply

Take each phrase in verses 78-79, thinking about how God has made each of these promises real to you through Jesus.

Christ in Christmas

Some of us seek to remove from our celebrations the excesses of eating, drinking and materialism that characterise a pagan Christmas.

Yet even having done so, we are still left far removed from the stark reality of the first Christmas.

The first Christmas

Read Luke 2:1-7

❷ *What are you most looking forward to on Christmas Day this coming Friday?*

❷ *What do you notice about the way this story is told?*

Without ceremony, and in complete obscurity, the Son of God enters the world—the place of his birth determined by the decree of a distant emperor, who proclaimed himself God. And yet, unknown, the great Augustus was doing the bidding of the one true God as Jesus is born in Bethlehem, just as the Scriptures foretold.

⌄ Apply

It is all too easy to leave Christ out of Christmas...

❷ *Beyond the traditions and family fun, how should these truths shape how we think about Christmas?*

❷ *What attitudes and behaviour do you need to pray to avoid?*

❷ *What practical measures can you take to rejoice in Jesus' birth in a fitting way this Christmas? Write your ideas in the space to the right.*

Look again at verse 7. Think of that love. Think of that poverty. And think of the incalculable riches which that poverty bought for you: "For you know the grace of our Lord Jesus Christ, that though he was rich, yet for your sake he became poor, so that you through his poverty might become rich" (2 Corinthians 8:9).

The manger was just the beginning of his poverty. A life of loneliness and grief, ending in a death of unutterable sorrow and desolation. That is the true measure of his love.

⌃ Pray

Enjoy your Christmas! But pray that you won't let the laughter and fun drown out this message of Jesus' love. Don't let your heart be so crowded out with other things that, like the inn, there is no room for him.

First responders

Mary sang that in Jesus, God would fill "the hungry with good things". We see that starkly illustrated as the message of his birth goes out to a bunch of poor nobodies.

Isaiah's prophecy about Jesus says, "The Spirit of the Sovereign LORD is on me, because the LORD has anointed me to proclaim good news to the poor. He has sent me to bind up the broken-hearted..." (Isaiah 61:1).

Not first to kings, politicians, the wealthy and privileged, nor even to priests and the religious elite. But to poor, despised, ordinary shepherds.

To the poor

Read Luke 2:8-12

❓ *What is the shocking difference between the message (v 11) and the sign (v 12)?*

❓ *What three objections to Christianity are countered in verse 10?*

It is good news, not bad; life in Christ is joyful, not miserable; and the message is for *all* people—not just the religious-minded. What a great message this is!

⌄ Apply

There are many poor, despised, lonely, sad, unloved people on Christmas day. Christmas seems especially bleak to them; perhaps it does to you? It is people like this that Jesus came to save from sin. Pray that the good news of Jesus, the Saviour, will flood such hearts with intense joy, transforming their lives with Christ's love. And why not knock on doors down your street to invite people who may be isolated to join you?

Praise!

Christmas is not only a time for great joy but for great praise too.

Read Luke 2:13-14

❓ *What precisely do the angels praise God for?*

It is understandable that we get tired of singing carols by this stage of the Christmas season, but have you begun yet to lift your voice in heartfelt praise to God for his wonderful gift to you? The shepherds listen in wonder to this dazzling display of heaven's praise for God's work of reconciliation.

⌄ Apply

Is there any practical way you can show the love of Christ to sad and lonely people this Christmas? There may be many who are alone, bereaved, or struggling with isolation.

It's easy as well, to just mechanically "join in" with Christmas carols on autopilot. Determine that you will pause for a moment to tune your heart to praise God before you open your mouth to sing.

"Thank yous" are not always sincere at Christmas. Can you be sincere now as you say your "thank you" for his greatest gift: genuine peace for those who receive the righteousness of Christ?

A song for dark days

The psalms not only engage us intellectually but also emotionally. We are people who are created to feel, as well as think. Wonderfully, God's word understands this.

Read Psalm 42 (slowly)

I am panting

❓ *Have you experienced something of the feelings of the writer in verses 1-3?*

One way to describe what he is going through is spiritual depression. It's caused inwardly, by a feeling of distance from God (v 1-2); and externally, through people mocking his faith even as the tears well up (v 3).

❓ *How does he feel treated by God (v 7, 9)?*

❓ *What does he remember (v 4)?*

❓ *Do you think looking back like this would make him feel better, or worse?*

So much of life is hard. So many of us are struggling. So often we wrestle with circumstances we would not choose and cannot change. We know what it is to sink into sadness, or slide deeper towards depression. And we know what it is to ask God, whether in a whisper of despair or a shout of rage, "Why have you forgotten me?" (v 9).

And if you are feeling like this today, this psalm says to you: it is okay to feel like this. That's actually quite liberating.

But that's not this psalm's last word...

I will praise him

❓ *Who does the writer address in verses 5 and 11?*

❓ *What does he tell them?*

❓ *How does he describe God (v 4, 9, 11)?*

The writer does not deny what he is feeling about life—but neither does he forget what he knows is true about God. And because he knows who God is, he knows he will not always feel like this. A day will come when "I will yet praise him"—even though that day does not seem to be today.

And so he talks to himself. He tells himself about who God is. Talking to yourself as a Christian isn't a sign of madness—it's a sign of maturity. We remind ourselves that God is greater than our feelings, and sovereign over our circumstances (they are his waterfalls, v 7). We remind ourselves that God has set before us a future where, with restored minds and hearts in renewed bodies in a recreated world, standing before the throne of our Saviour, we will "praise him".

Without God, we would be left with only tears for company (v 3). With him, we know hope, even as we well up. This is how we deal with spiritual depression, and how we respond when the tears won't stop. It is okay to feel like this. But there is no need to be dominated by this. I will yet praise God.

⌃ Pray

❓ *Do you need to speak to yourself about God, and then speak to God about your feelings?*

Finding Christ

It is one thing to hear the good news and believe it to be true. It is quite another to go to Jesus and to know him for yourself.

Short search

Read Luke 2:15-16

Those who seek will find Jesus just as God has promised. But those who find will also have their lives changed by a living encounter with Jesus. The shepherds would go back to their sheep, but they had been transformed by their experience.

Shared message

Read Luke 2:17-19

❓ *What do they immediately do next?*

❓ *Precisely what was the message they passed on (v 17, see v 10-11)?*

❓ *Why is this precision in their message important, do you think?*

❓ *What kind of things do you think Mary was pondering in her heart?*

Seeing the child just as they had been told was enough to convince them. Now the shepherds could be sure that this was the Messiah, the Saviour, as the angel had said. But they could not keep the fantastic news to themselves; at the risk of being ridiculed for spinning such a yarn, they broadcast the truth about Jesus.

Witnessing is far from easy. But often it is how we live which makes the real impact. Surely we will not want to keep such life-giving news to ourselves! You may have only been a Christian for a short while.

Your understanding of the Bible may be shaky. But hasn't God done certain things in your life that you are sure of? Hasn't he convinced you of a few life-changing truths? Tell others what God has done for you, even if you can go no further.

Praising God

Read Luke 2:20

❓ *What is the difference, do you think, between glorifying and praising God?*

They rushed to see the truth for themselves. They returned with praise at the wonder of that truth. It's a simple enough chain of events. They heard. They saw. They told. They worshipped.

❓ *Which of these elements of experiencing Christ is most lacking in your Christian life today?*

Pray

Pray for courage to run the risk of looking stupid as you tell others about what you have heard and seen. Isn't it better to look and feel a little foolish than for others not to realise that Jesus is both Saviour and Lord?

Pray that God would use your faltering testimony to have a similar effect as the shepherds' words. Some who heard were amazed. But at least one who heard remembered all these things, turning them over in her mind.

The law of the Lord

As Jews, Jesus and his parents kept the requirements of the Old Testament law. As he said later, Jesus had not come to destroy the law but to fulfil it perfectly.

Keeping it

Read Luke 2:21-24

❷ *Which two rituals did Jesus go through in obedience to the law?*

❷ *What spiritual significance do these rites have for us today?*

❷ *How will Jesus fulfil both in his life, death and resurrection?*

❷ *What does the name "Jesus" mean?*

Not only did Jesus keep God's law to the letter but he also fulfilled the spiritual meaning of God's requirements for his people. The law pointed to Christ and his new spiritual kingdom. Now Christ has come, the need for keeping ceremonial law is over…

Circumcision (v 21) possibly indicated that sin needed to be "cut away" for a child to be part of the Lord's family of Israel. Jesus had no sin, but he came to remove the sins of others. Believers today have been circumcised, not literally, but by God's Spirit, in their hearts. By God's grace, we have been set apart from our sin and have that mark of belonging to the Lord's family.

Purification (v 22, 24) took place after 40 days. All that time had to pass before a woman who had given birth could once again worship God in the temple. Until then, her discharges made her ceremonially unclean. For purification there must be sacrifice (v 24). For Mary, the text makes clear that this was the poor person's offering of two doves.

Dedication (v 23) to the Lord was expected, but the child could be redeemed by payment. Yes, the Redeemer was "redeemed"! Redemption money (5 shekels) must be paid for the firstborn son, instead of giving the child to the Lord's service (for he belonged to the Lord by right). This pointed to the redemption price that Jesus paid later to purchase his people. Christians have been redeemed at the price of Jesus' blood. And so we belong to the Lord as his son or daughter!

Do we sufficiently grasp the importance of purity before a holy God? The Old Testament laws were so particular about uncleanness—and purification was a long and costly process. Praise God that Jesus came to completely wash away sin; in Jesus, believers are pure and blameless.

⌄ Apply

The "law of the Lord" for Christians to follow is the law of love; Christ has fulfilled the demands of the law for us, so we may freely serve him and follow his ways.

❷ *Are you showing your gratitude? What opportunities will the next 72 hours give you to do so?*

A song for Christmas

Happy Christmas! Have a great day, and know something of the joy of the Christmas gospel. You probably have a full day ahead (or behind) so enjoy this song of joy.

Truly spiritual

Read Luke 2:25-27

> ❷ *What kind of man is Simeon?*
>
> ❷ *What do you think it means that Jesus would be the "consolation" of Israel?*

Simeon, like many godly Jews, had been longing to see the Messiah, who would bring consolation to Israel (see Isaiah 40:1-2)— that is, comfort and guidance. Unlike others, Simeon knew that he would see him. Here was a man of God. His whole life was focused on living right and waiting patiently. Even before the age of the Spirit, Simeon was blessed with the Holy Spirit in his life. Imagine Simeon's immense joy to discover his Saviour in the temple!

Truly remarkable

Read Luke 2:28-33

> ❷ *What is truly remarkable about Simeon's song of praise?*

A stunning insight that left his parents astonished. While others found it hard to come to terms with Old Testament prophecies promising that the Messiah would bless the despised Gentiles, this truth was a delight to Simeon—a matter for praise and wonder.

Not surprisingly, Joseph and Mary were amazed. But there were more truths to come that would make them think long and hard about this child...

A piercing sword

Read Luke 2:34-35

> ❷ *What does Simeon mean by these cryptic statements?*
>
> ❷ *How would Mary have responded to them, do you think?*

Some of the phrases are hard to understand, but the drift is clear. Simeon was already looking beyond the glory of the gift of Jesus, the Saviour—he could begin to see the pain and sorrow Jesus would suffer, the division and the heart-searching he would bring, the grief his death would mean for Mary.

✓ Apply

Could Simeon see, by faith, the reason for all this? Could he see salvation by the death of Jesus on the cross? We cannot tell. But this much is sure: Simeon had seen enough to be ready to rest in peace—to rest in Jesus as his Saviour—even as the child rested in his arms.

> ❷ *Have you seen enough in Jesus to know that death can now be embraced with joy, rather than feared?*

⌃ Pray

Give thanks that today you celebrate a light of revelation to the whole world. Pray that the light of Jesus would illuminate all that happens today.

Prayerful prophetess

Always busy at the church, often up at night praying, spends whole days fasting... This sounds like a description of an energetic young Christian, but is in fact an 84-year old!

All out for God

Read Luke 2:36-38

❷ *Why is there so much detail about Anna's life and family, do you think?*

❷ *What do we learn about her character and priorities?*

❷ *Having seen Jesus, what does she do?*

Exactly how old Anna was is debated. The point is that she was very old, but very devoted; still full of commitment to God.

Paul encourages us to "pray continually" (1 Thessalonians 5:17). Anna seems almost literally to have done that, from the description in Luke 2:37. Maybe she had a room within the temple complex, or perhaps it is just a figurative way to describe her regularity ("she's always there!"). Either way, Anna devoted a great deal of time to prayer.

⌄ Apply

If you are still young, don't you find Anna's example a great challenge? You have far more energy—but how much of it is directed towards serving God?

If you are older, what an encouragement to think that, however weak you may be, prayer is counted as serving God.

Answered prayer

Read Luke 2:38 again

❷ *What do you think is meant by the phrase "redemption of Jerusalem"?*

Prayer is not just a holy way of spending time. God had answered Anna's pleading for God to come and visit his people, to revive them, to send the Messiah to save them. There were just a few who were still looking and praying for the "redemption of Jerusalem"—now she could see the Redeemer with her own eyes.

⌃ Pray

"But we have our jobs to do, school to go to, family to care for. We can't always be praying as Anna did..."

True. But we can do everything in a prayerful attitude. We can keep our thoughts shooting up to God, conscious of his presence, relying on his help, thanking him for his goodness. And when we have to wait for something, or when our mind does not need to be occupied, we can talk to the Lord about the things on our hearts—but more importantly, the things we know are on *his* heart.

NAHUM: Meet God

To finish the year, we have a short series in one of the lesser-known "minor prophets": Nahum.

---

❷ *If you were writing a personality profile of God, what would you say were his main character traits?*

Who, where, when?

Read Nahum 1:1

Assyria (with its capital of Nineveh) is clearly a world power at this time (i.e. 7th-century BC). Nineveh is renowned in the Bible for its wickedness (Jonah 1:2).

The character of God

Read Nahum 1:2-3

❷ *Verses 2-3 explain the character of God. What words can you pick out to describe his character?*

Creator and judge

Read Nahum 1:4-8

Verses 4-6 focus on God as Creator. At the beginning and at the end of these verses, the focus is on inanimate creation (i.e. sea, mountains, earth, rocks). In the middle, the focus falls on humans. With both, God is able to do as he pleases.

Re-read Nahum 1:7-8

❷ *What pleases our good God, and how will he act towards those who trust him?*

❷ *What displeases our good God, and what will he do with those who set themselves against him?*

These verses are a great summary of the central message of Nahum. God cares for (literally "knows") those who trust him, but at the same time he is a warrior towards his opponents.

This portrait of God is known to those who know him through Jesus. On the cross, God does exactly what is envisioned here. He fights against the enemies of his people while caring for and rescuing those who put their faith in Jesus.

Read Nahum 1:9-10

❷ *If God really is as verses 7-8 say, what will that look like for wicked Nineveh?*

⌃ Pray

Thank God that he is both firm on evil and on those who do it and that he loves, knows and protects those who love him. Pray that God would act according to his word here in Nahum for his persecuted people around the world.

Speaking directly

Having laid out principles for action, God now speaks directly to his wicked enemy. He will act according to his nature.

The reason for God's words

Read Nahum 1:11

A person has "come forth" from Nineveh.

❷ *What are they noted for?*

❷ *Against whom are their actions directed?*

Read Nahum 1:15

Verse 11 spoke of wicked plans.

❷ *How is that wickedness being expressed on this occasion?*

Notice how personal and direct this accusation is. God has seen the evil of this nation. It is against him. He is against them.

God's first word

Read Nahum 1:12-13

In verses 7-8, we saw two different groups of people: those who trust God, and those who set themselves against him. Now God addresses both groups separately (Judah in verses 12-13 and Nineveh in verses 14-15). Complete each sentence.

Although Nineveh looks so strong...

Although God has afflicted Judah in the past, now he will...

and...

God's second word

Read Nahum 1:14

God's word to Judah had three parts, and so does his word to Nineveh.

❷ *What three promises/commands are given?*

Great news

Read Nahum 1:15

❷ *What great news will a runner bring to God's people?*

❷ *What is God's promise to them?*

❷ *How should they respond?*

Many of us find it hard that God's goodness (v 7) can be expressed both in love and in destruction. However, that may be because for humans, violence cannot easily be separated from human vindictiveness and caprice. But God is not like this, which is why we can leave judgment to him (see Romans 12:19-21).

⌃ Pray

Thank God that he is a good judge who justly deals with evil and whose mercy triumphs over judgment. Praise him that he is the author of the even greater news of salvation and forgiveness in Jesus. Pray for those you know who struggle to believe that God is good.

Friends and enemies

God's people are sometimes brutalised by human and other forces. Nevertheless, our future is secure.

A summons to the Lord's enemies

Read Nahum 2:1

❷ *From the context, who do you think the unnamed attacker is in these verses?*

❷ *What orders are given to the inhabitants?*

The picture here is of a city under siege, setting up defences in the hope of defending itself against breach. The ESV's translation of "scatterer" is better than "attacker".

The result of the Lord's intervention

Read Nahum 2:3-7

❷ *What will be the result for the besieged enemy of God? How successful will their defences be?*

❷ *Who is responsible for the defeat, do you think?*

Notice the reference to God's decree in verse 7. God's word controls what happens in God's world. While that word can be creative, and can decree salvation (e.g. Genesis 1; 12:1-3; 2 Corinthians 4:6), it can also pronounce judgment on his enemies—as it does here.

Read Nahum 2:2

❷ *What will be the result for the persecuted people of God?*

Notice that in this passage only two parties are named in the same verse (v 2): "the LORD" and "Jacob". The force of this is to bind the two together.

The Bible testifies that God's people are not always spared trouble (e.g. verse 2: "destroyers have laid them waste and have ruined their vines"). However, because they belong to God, he will ultimately restore them and overcome their enemies.

⌄ Apply

❷ *When do you most need to remember this in your life?*

❷ *Is there a Christian you know who needs you to remind them of this today?*

⌃ Pray

The Lord's Prayer (Matthew 6:9-13) identifies God's goal: the hallowing of his name, the doing of his will and the coming of his kingdom. However, the Christian faces threats to this (see the second half of the prayer). Included in these is evil. Yet in and through Christ, the devil is defeated and God loves and protects his people.

Pray now, thanking God for the bond forged in Christ between himself and his people, and that it can never be broken.

God is a warrior

What do you think about images of God as a warrior? Are they Christian? Are they helpful? Can we thank God for being a warrior? Yes!

Images of defeated Nineveh

Read Nahum 2:8-10

In verse 8, Nineveh is linked to a ruptured pool of water. The fleeing waters refer to her fleeing defenders.

❷ *What are the marks of a defeated city outlined in verses 8-10?*

The lion hunt

Read Nahum 2:11-13

❷ *If the Assyrian king and his court are likened to a lion and his den, what is the main point of verses 11-13?*

❷ *How will the Lord Almighty respond to such conduct?*

Woe to the city of bloodshed

Read Nahum 3:1-3

These verses contain a woe oracle (often marked in English by words such as "Ah!" or "Woe!"). Such oracles are not so much expressions of grief, but rather, ways of expressing anger.

❷ *What main charges are levelled against Nineveh? If you were writing a character assessment of the city, what words would you use?*

❷ *How will Nineveh's end match her own character and actions?*

A humiliated sorceress-prostitute

Read Nahum 3:4-7

The language in these verses is strong, and needs to be understood against its background culture. It was customary in the ancient Near East to compare cities to women. For Israel, the worst sort of women were prostitutes and sorceresses. Both broke social and religious norms and did so for money.

Both Old and New Testaments present God and his Son as warriors (e.g. Exodus 15:3; Revelation 19:11-16). However, there are differences. In the Old Testament, the enemies are the physical enemies of God and his people, whereas in the New Testament, the focus is on the spiritual forces of Satan and his cohorts (e.g. Colossians 2:14-15; Ephesians 4:7-10).

⌃ Pray

Thank God that he is protective of us, his people, and that his protective actions are for our good. Thank him for the victory won in and through Jesus. Thank him for his ongoing fighting over the forces of evil that would seek to draw his people away from their Lord Jesus.

Final words

What do you think God thinks of bad leaders? What should we pray for in relation to them?

Better than Thebes?

Read Nahum 3:8-11

❷ *What was the famous Thebes like? How did she end up?*

❷ *What should Nineveh learn from Thebes? How will Nineveh end up?*

Two illustrations

Read Nahum 3:12-13

❷ *What two illustrations are used in relation to Nineveh in these verses?*

❷ *What points are made by using these illustrations?*

A locust taunt

Read Nahum 3:15-17

Locust plagues were familiar in the ancient Near East. They were also used in prophetic imagery (if you have time, read Joel 1:2-12).

However, the imagery is used in a different way here. Here, Nineveh is urged to rapidly multiply its people like locusts to face the threat. Also, her leaders are like locusts who vacate quickly.

Final words

Read Nahum 3:18-19

In most of the prophecy, the city is addressed directly.

❷ *Who is now being addressed?*

❷ *What job are the rulers/nobles described as having (v 18: the footnote is helpful)?*

In biblical thought, these two roles are often linked. Rulers are to protect their people (e.g. 2 Samuel 5:1-5; Ezekiel 34). The king of Assyria and his nobles have spectacularly failed—and God will hold them accountable.

At one point in the ministry of Jesus, we are told that he sees people as sheep without a shepherd (Matthew 9:36). His answer in subsequent verses is to appoint the twelve to minister to them. Later he will call himself the good, true shepherd, who lays down his life for the sheep (John 10:1-18), and will appoint pastors and teachers to lead his people (Ephesians 4:11).

⌃ Pray

It is good for us to end these studies by praying for leadership around the world, particularly where it is harsh and brutal towards its people. We should by all means pray for God to turn the hearts of wicked rulers. However, if there is no repentance, then pray for the removal of wickedness. This would be consistent with God's message through Nahum. Pray for leadership in this way now, as well as any other encouragements or challenges you're taking from Nahum.

Bible in a year: Psalm 121

ROMANS FOR YOU SET

For Reading, for Feeding, for Leading

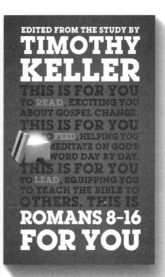

Join Dr Timothy Keller as he helps you to get to grips with the book of Romans, showing how it can transform our hearts and lives. Written for people of every age and stage, from new believers to pastors and teachers.

Introduce a friend to

explore

If you're enjoying using *Explore*, why not introduce a friend? Time with God is our introduction to daily Bible reading and is a great way to get started with a regular time with God. It includes 28 daily readings along with articles, advice and practical tips on how to apply what the passage teaches.

Why not order a copy for someone you would like to encourage?

Coming up next...

❤ Acts
with Matthew Hoskinson

❤ 1 Kings
with Dave Griffith-Jones

❤ Malachi
with Graham Beynon

❤ The Lord's Prayer
with Carl Laferton

Don't miss your copy. Contact your local Christian bookshop or church agent, or visit:

UK & Europe: thegoodbook.co.uk
info@thegoodbook.co.uk
Tel: 0333 123 0880

North America: thegoodbook.com
info@thegoodbook.com
Tel: 866 244 2165

Australia & New Zealand:
thegoodbook.com.au
info@thegoodbook.com.au
Tel: (02) 9564 3555

South Africa: www.christianbooks.co.za
orders@christianbooks.co.za
Tel: 021 674 6931/2